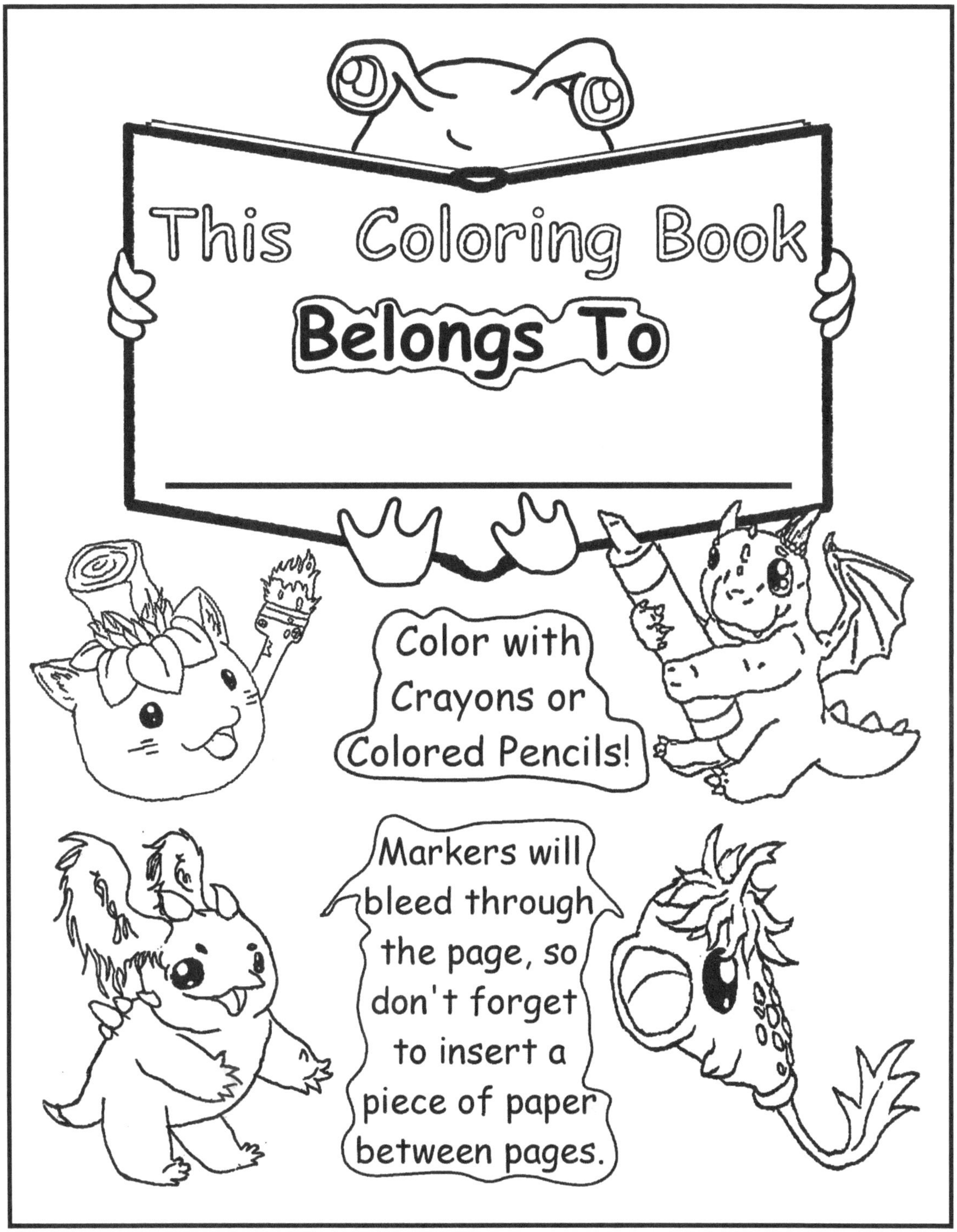

This Coloring Book **Belongs To**

_____

Color with Crayons or Colored Pencils!

Markers will bleed through the page, so don't forget to insert a piece of paper between pages.

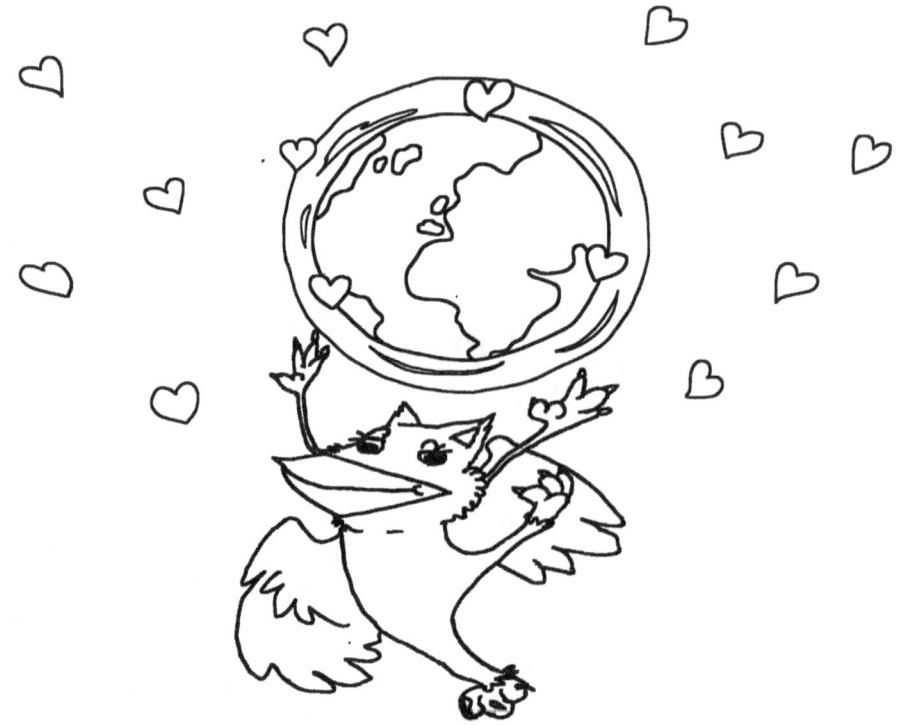

What inspired this coloring book?

I have always loved and enjoyed drawing since I can remember. But it's only a year ago that I found a cause for my art.

The storms that devastated so many lives and places made me want to do something. I realized I could make a coloring book and use it to raise money to help the World! Yes, Kids Can!

In this first series of 'I Draw, You Color!' you will find a mix of some of my old and recent artworks. I hope that a lot of kids and young at heart will have fun coloring my art.

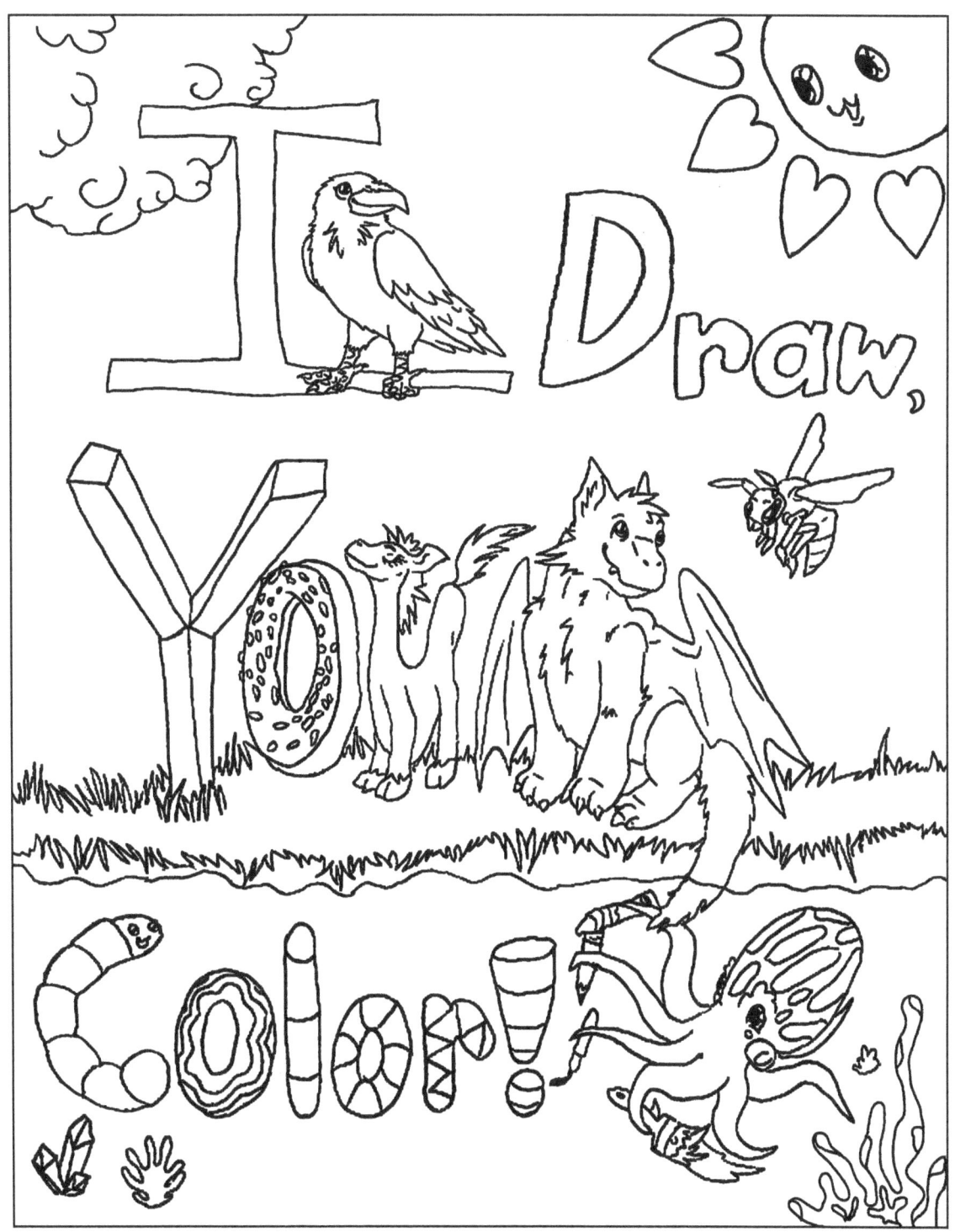

I Draw, Your Color!

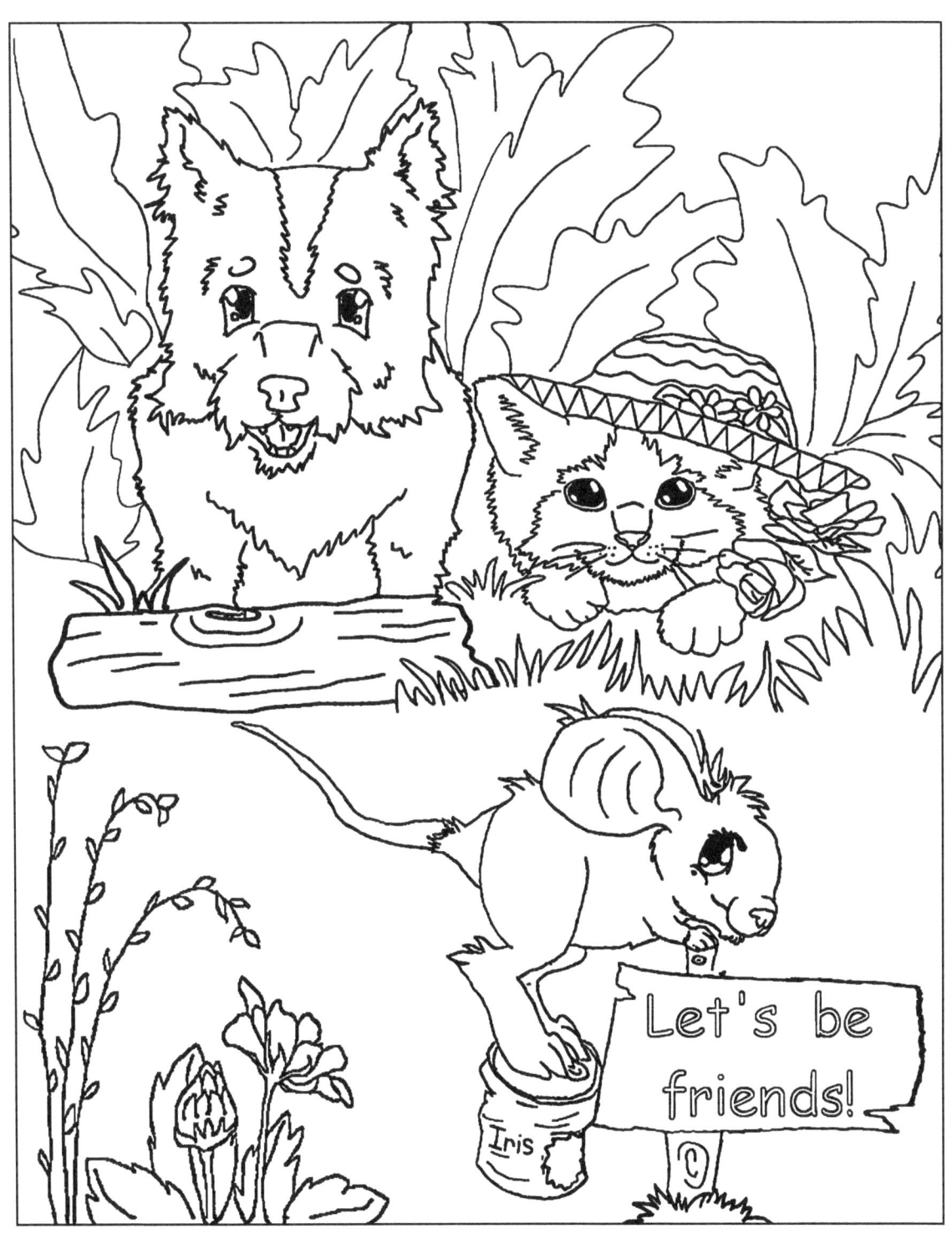

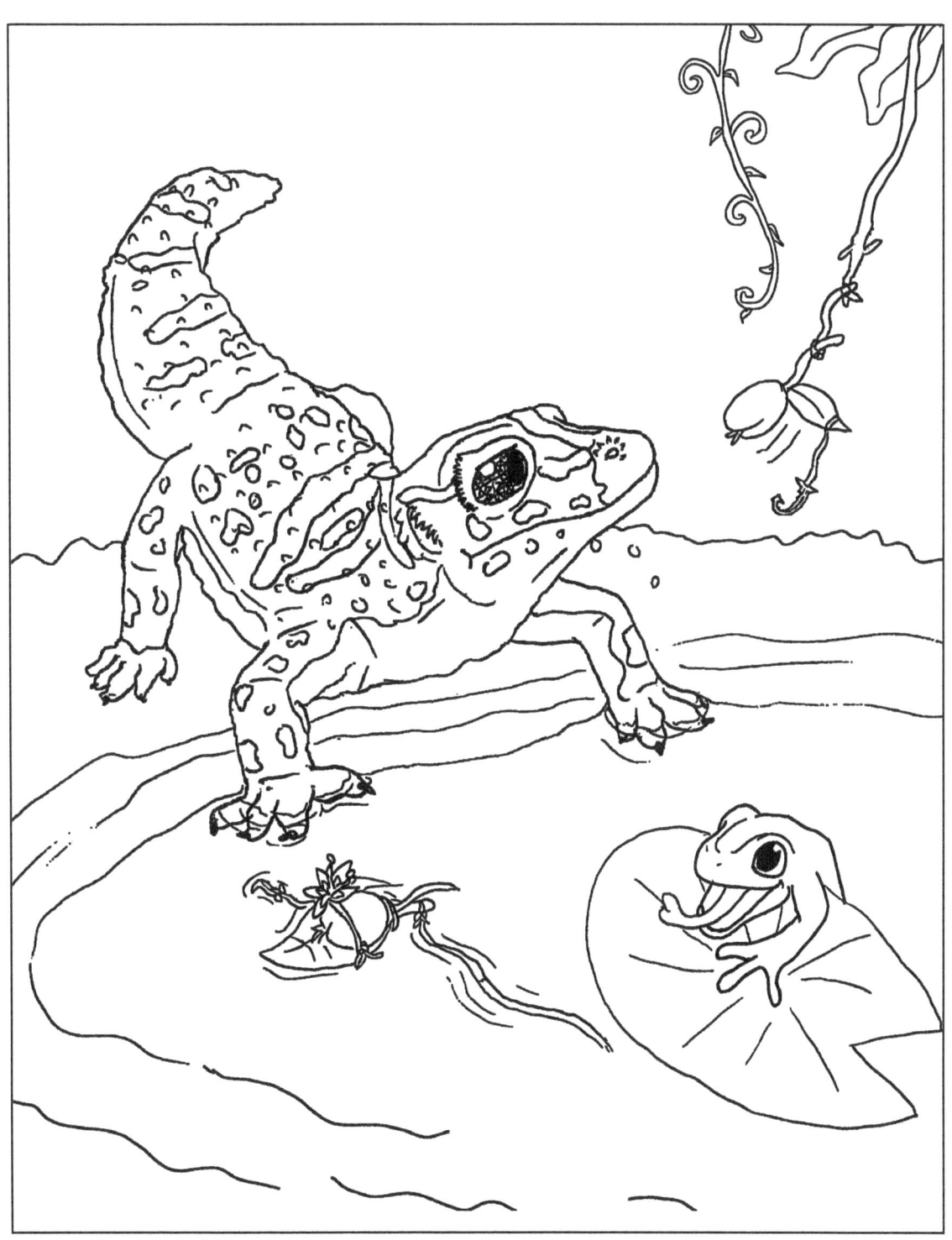

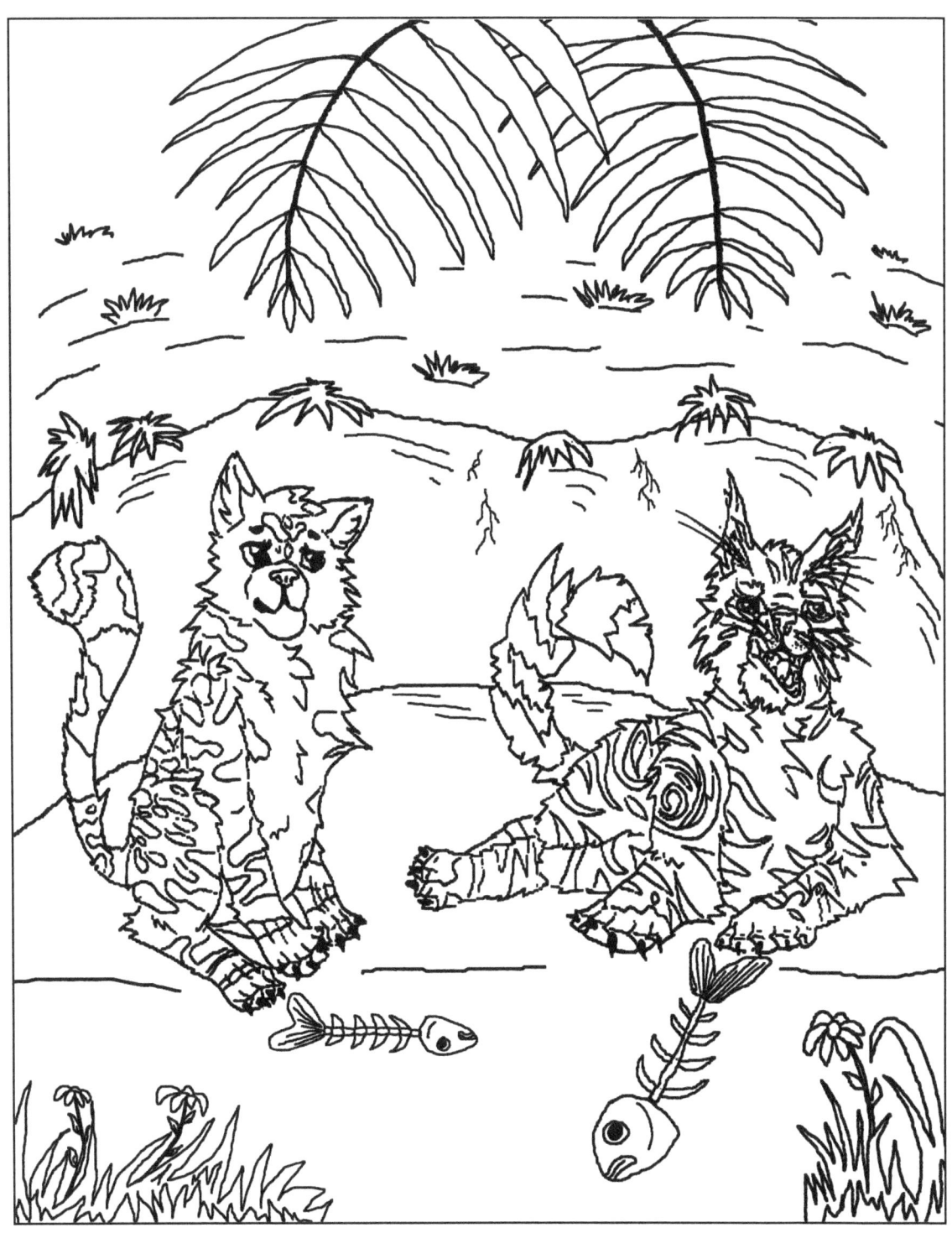

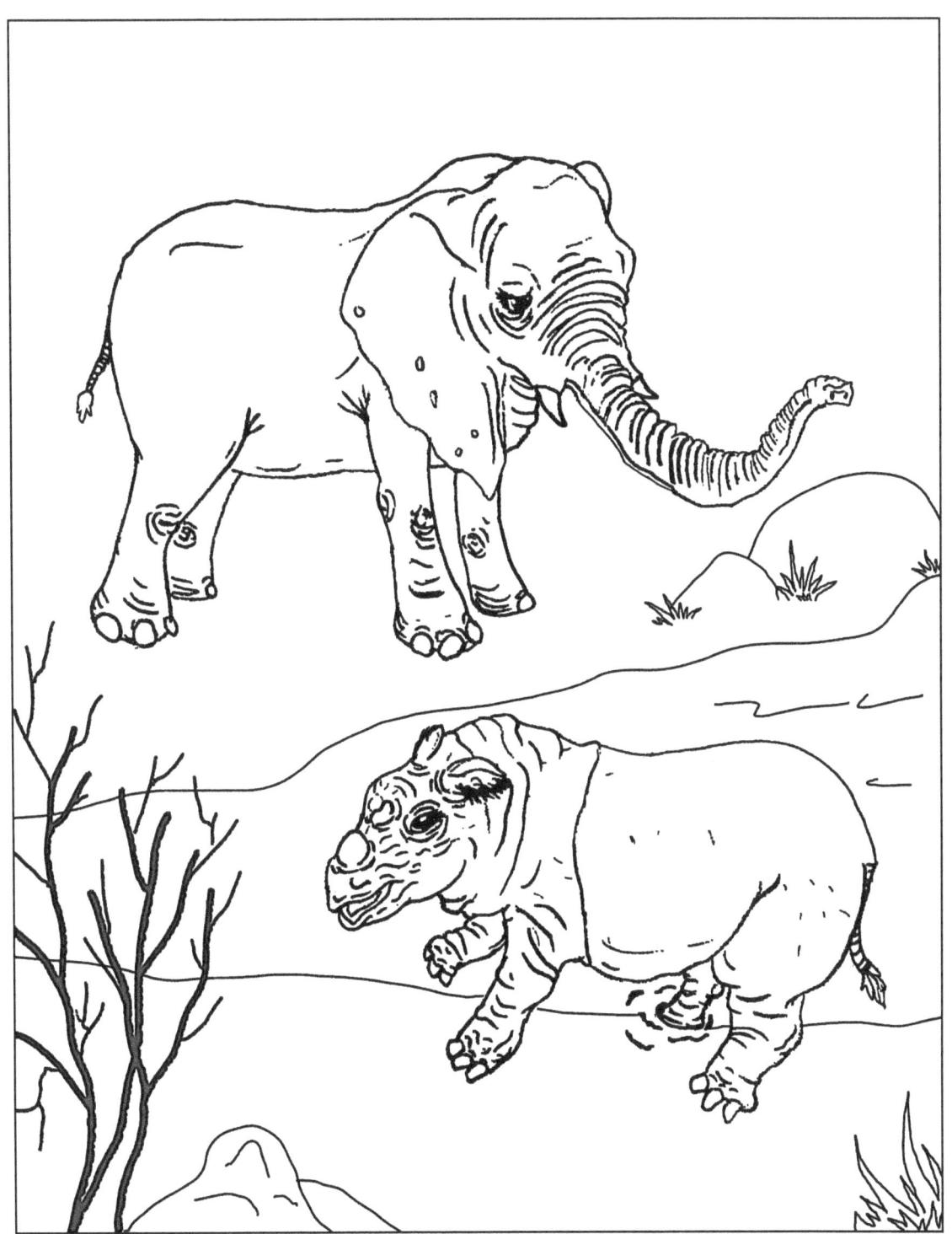

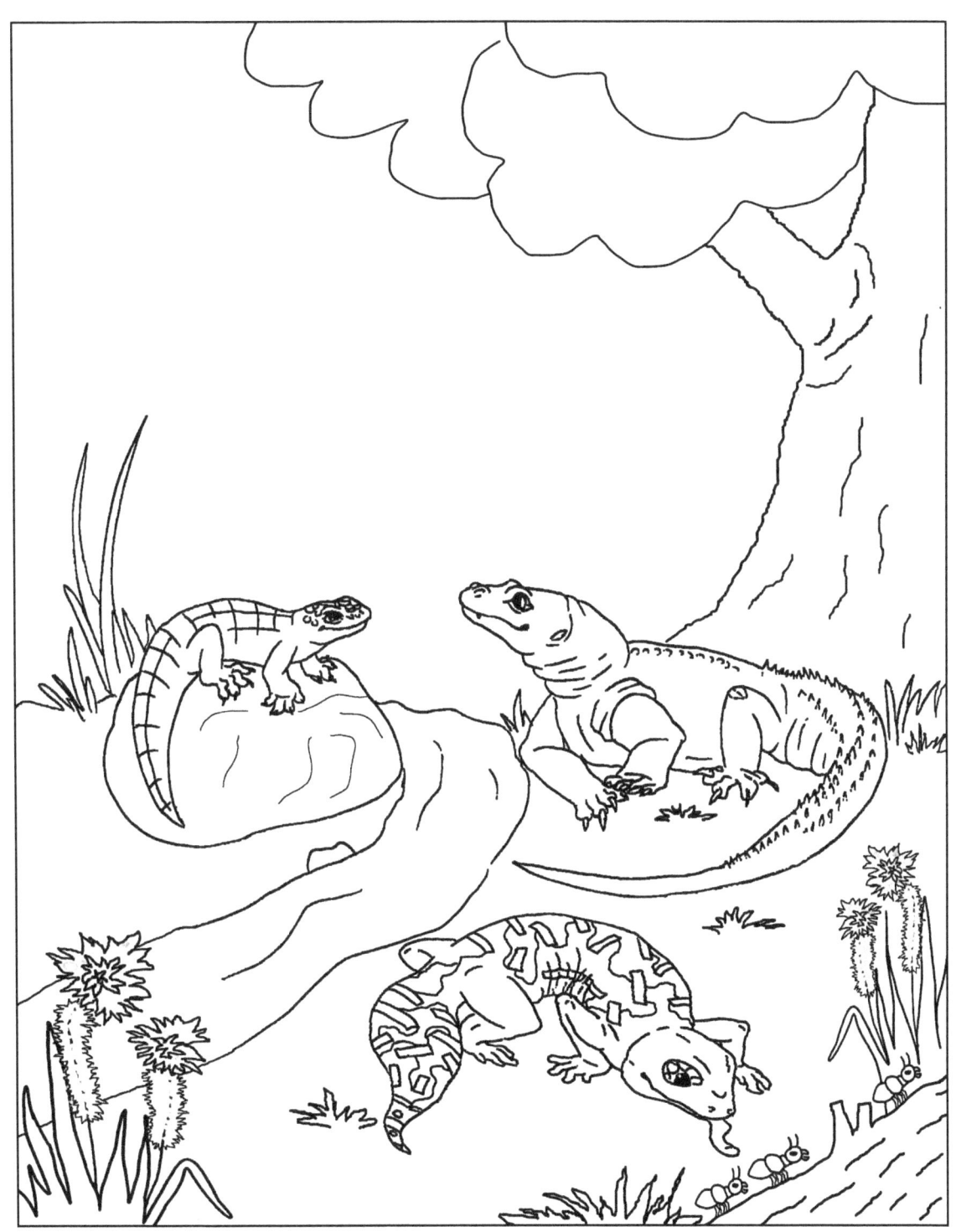

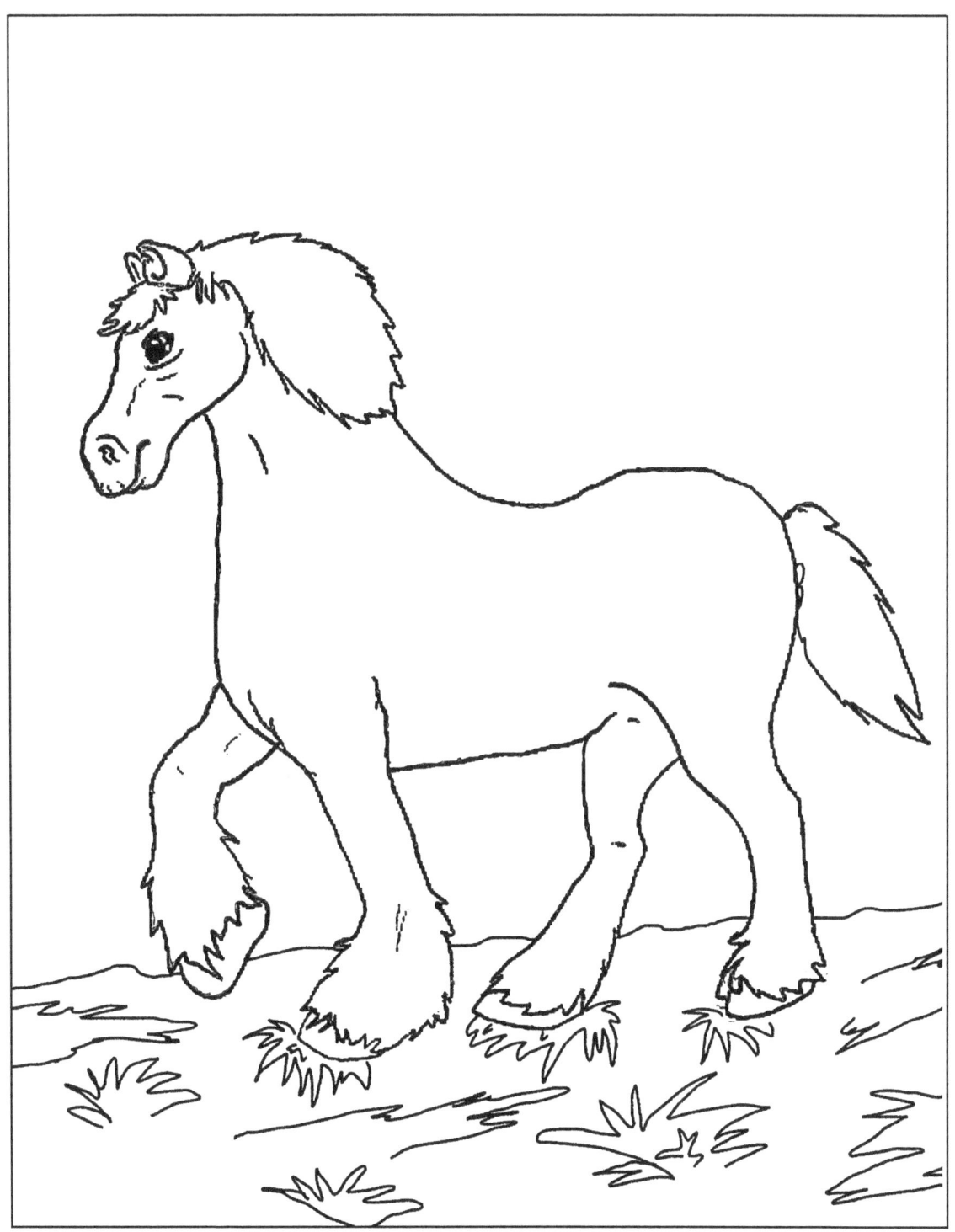

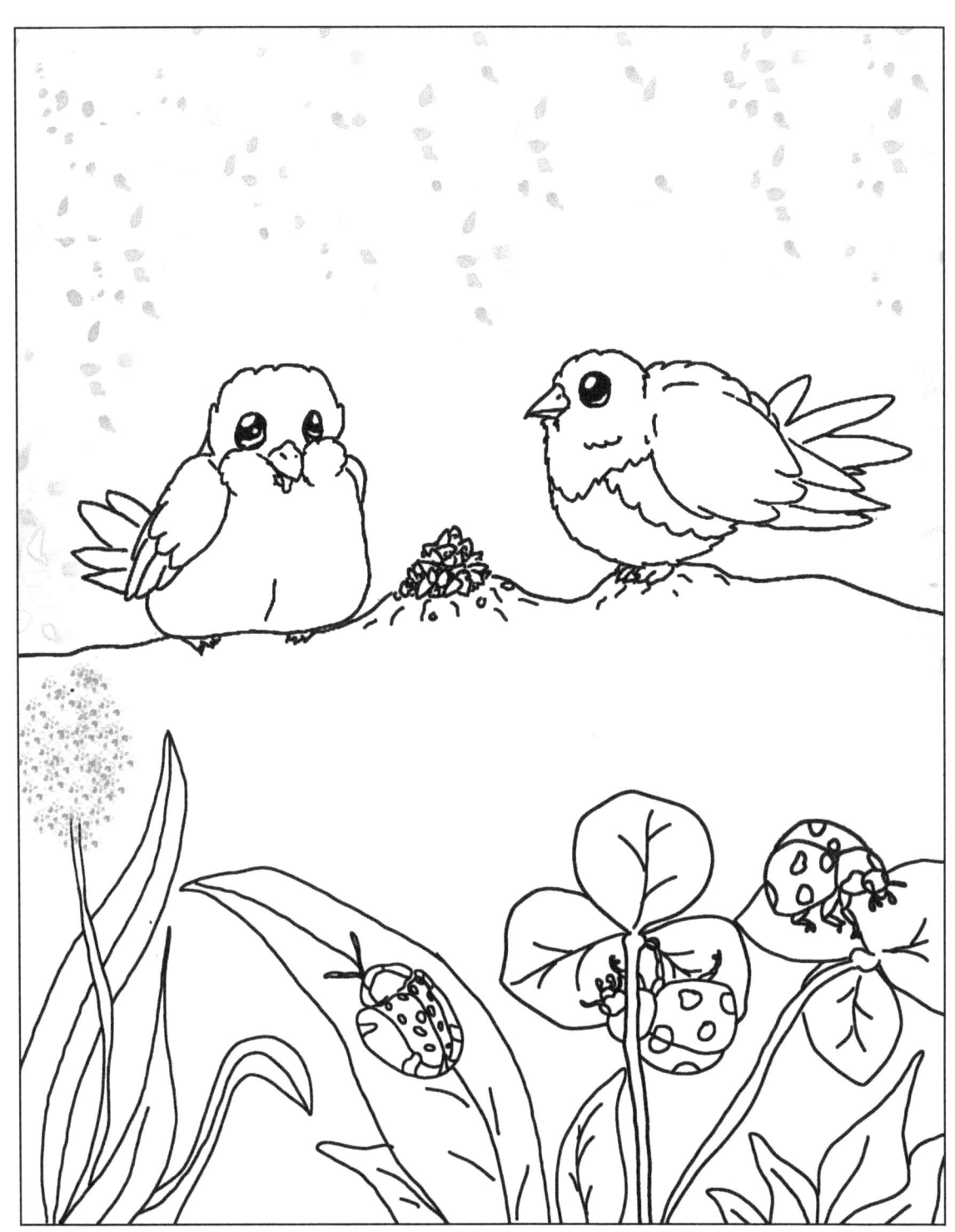

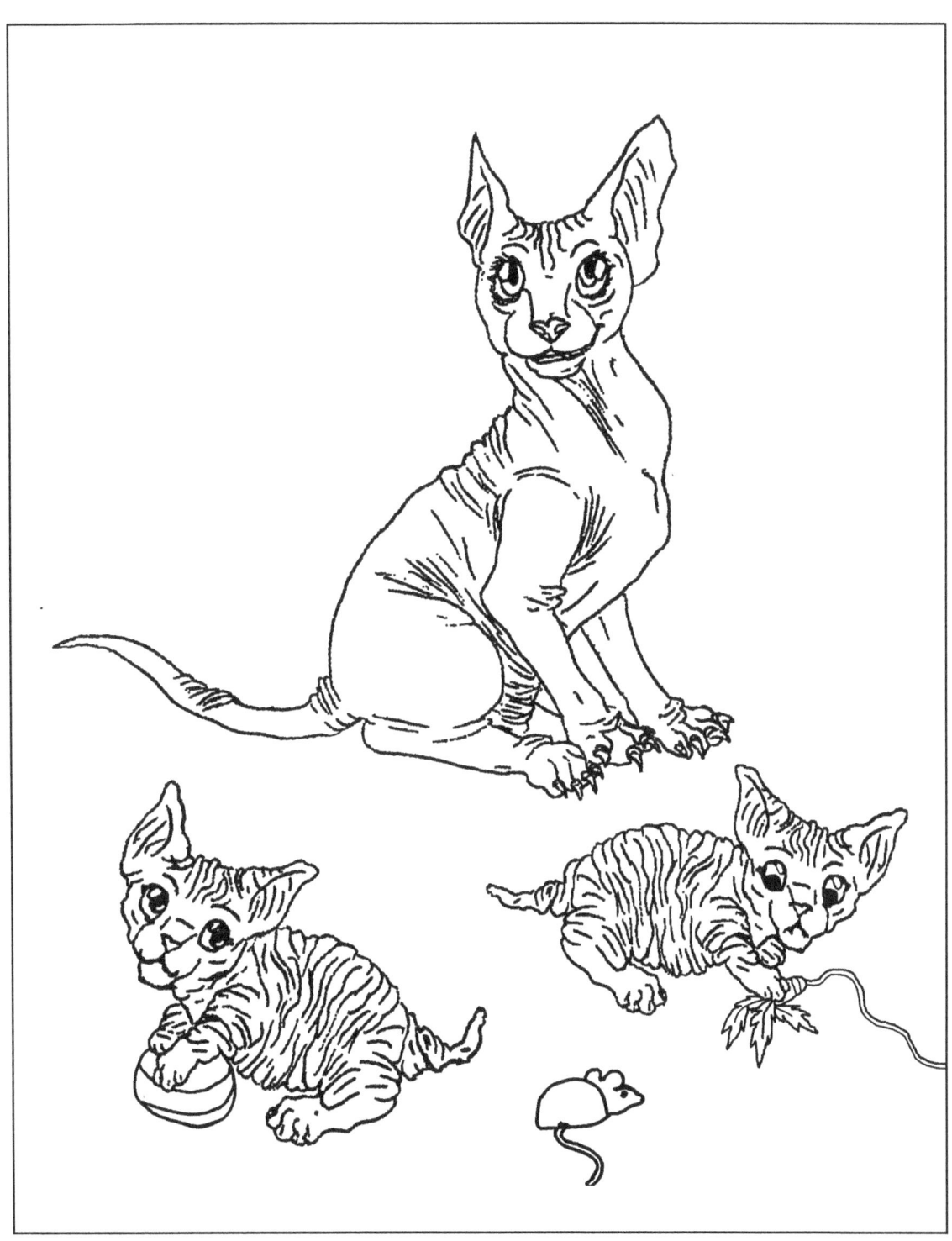

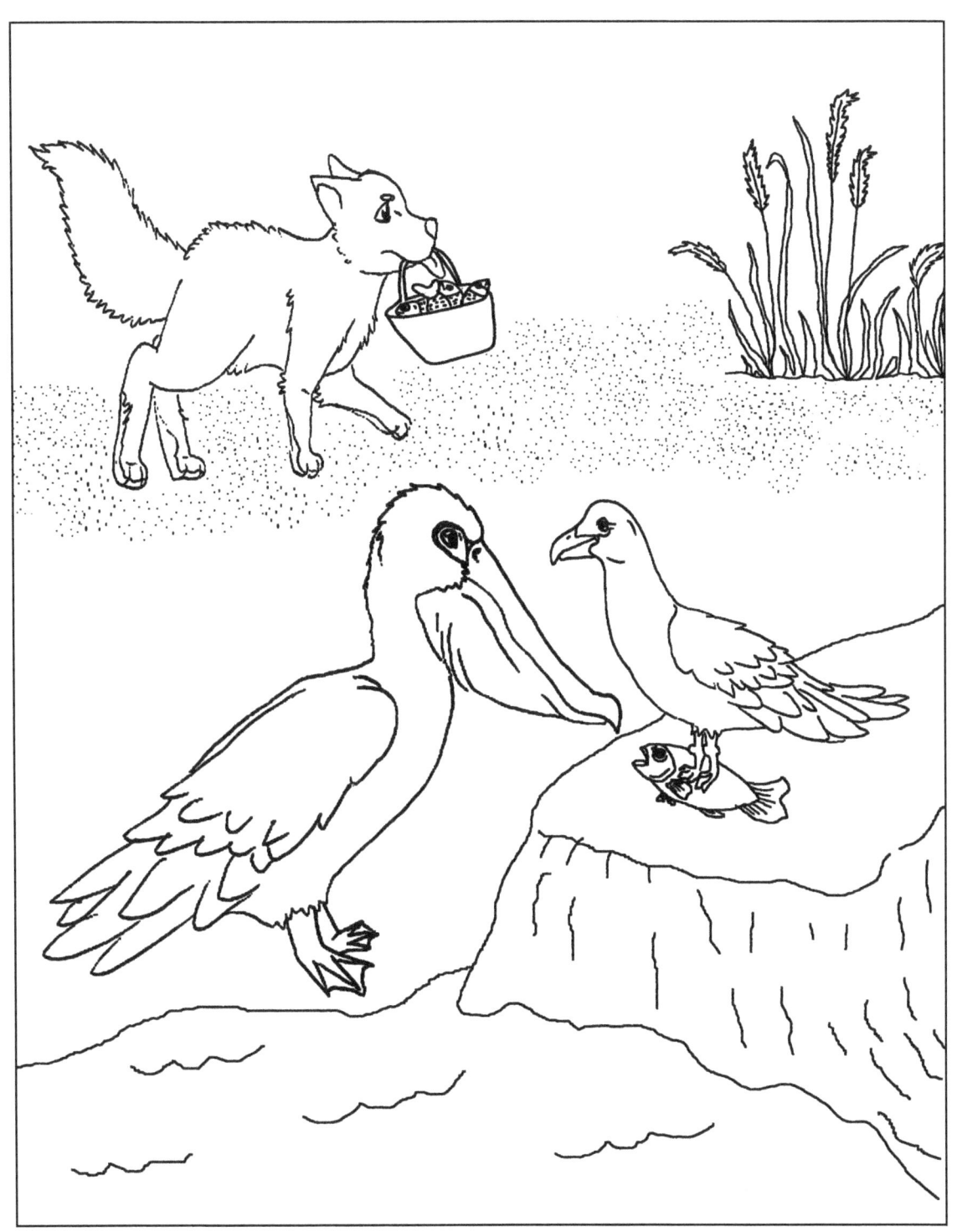

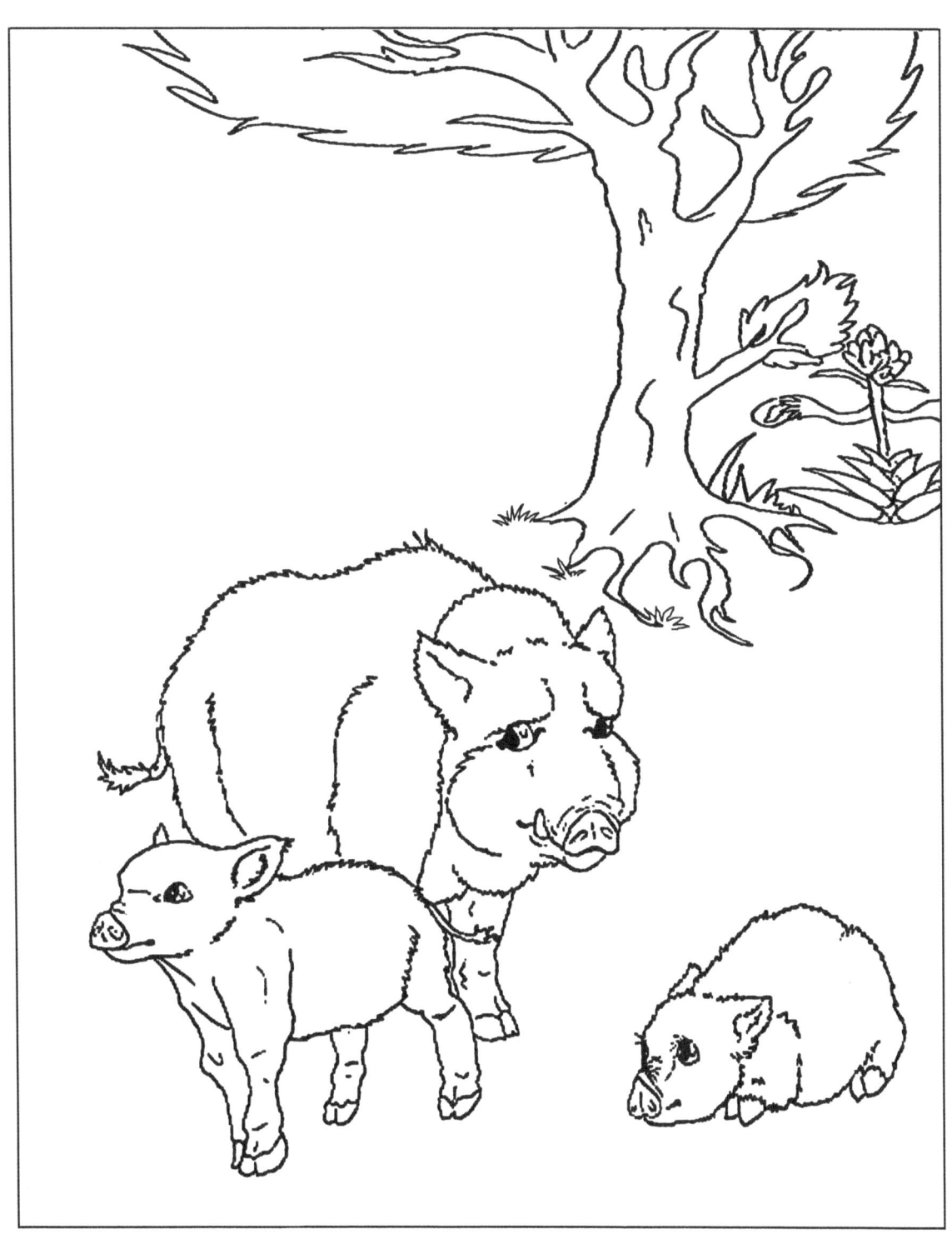

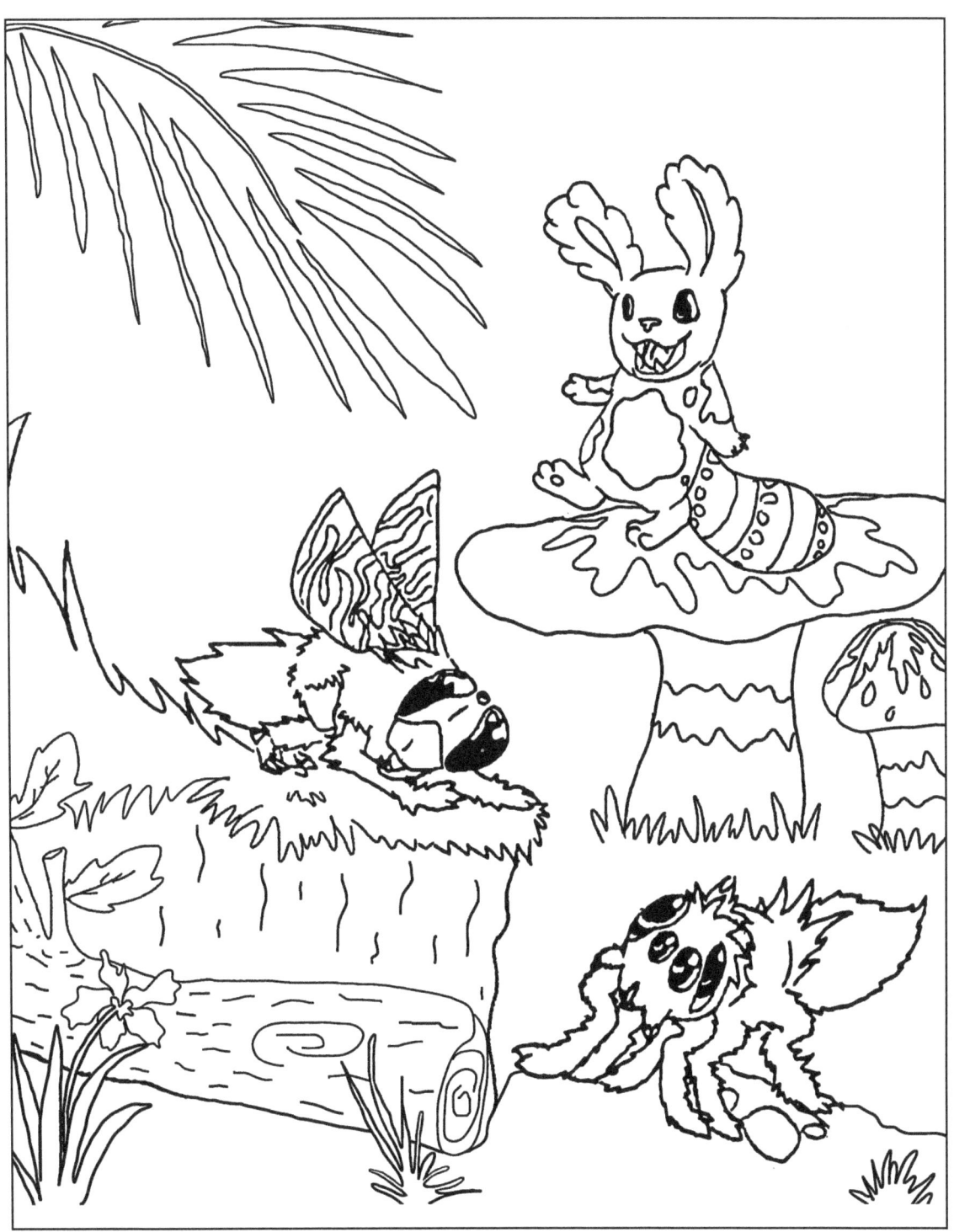

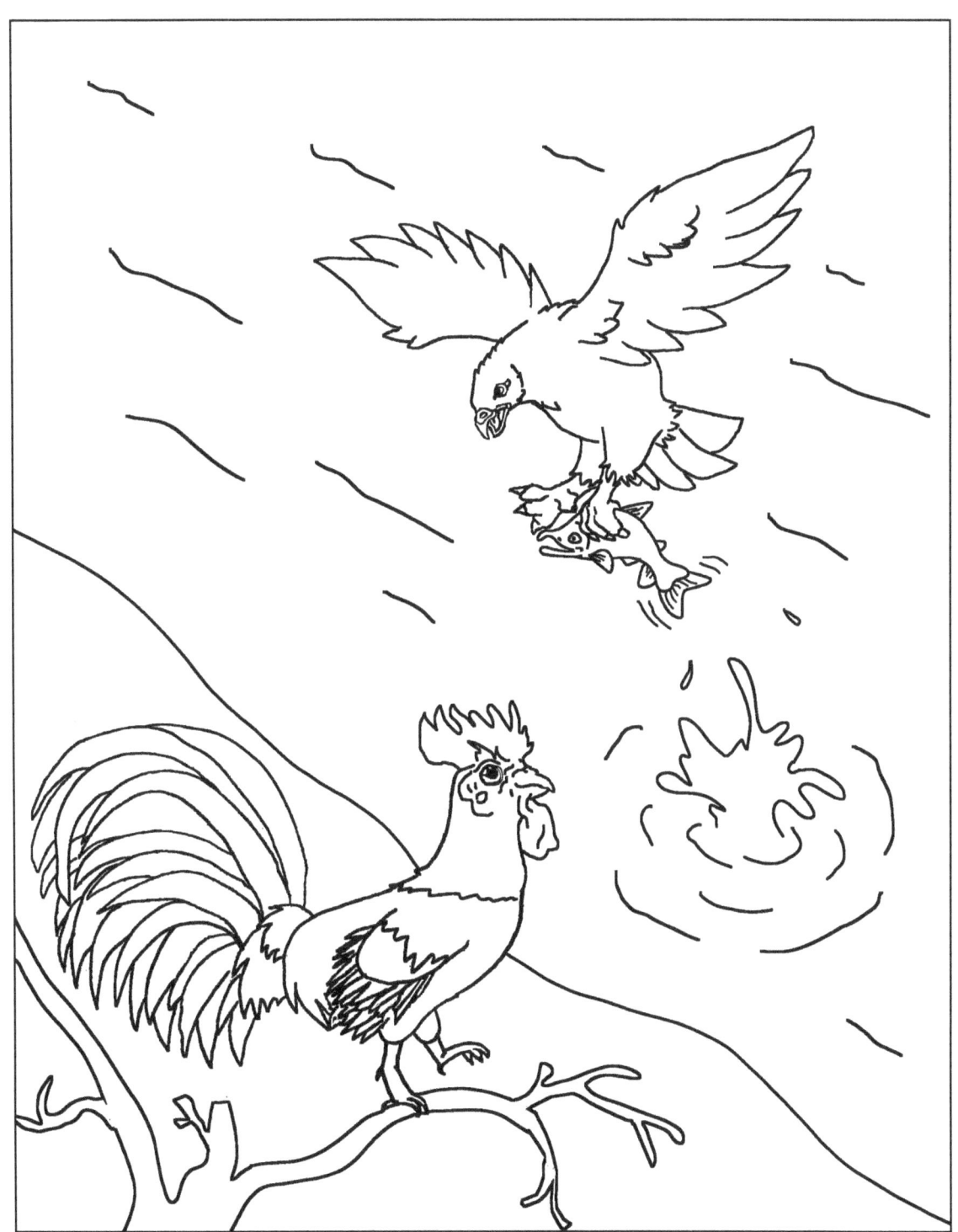

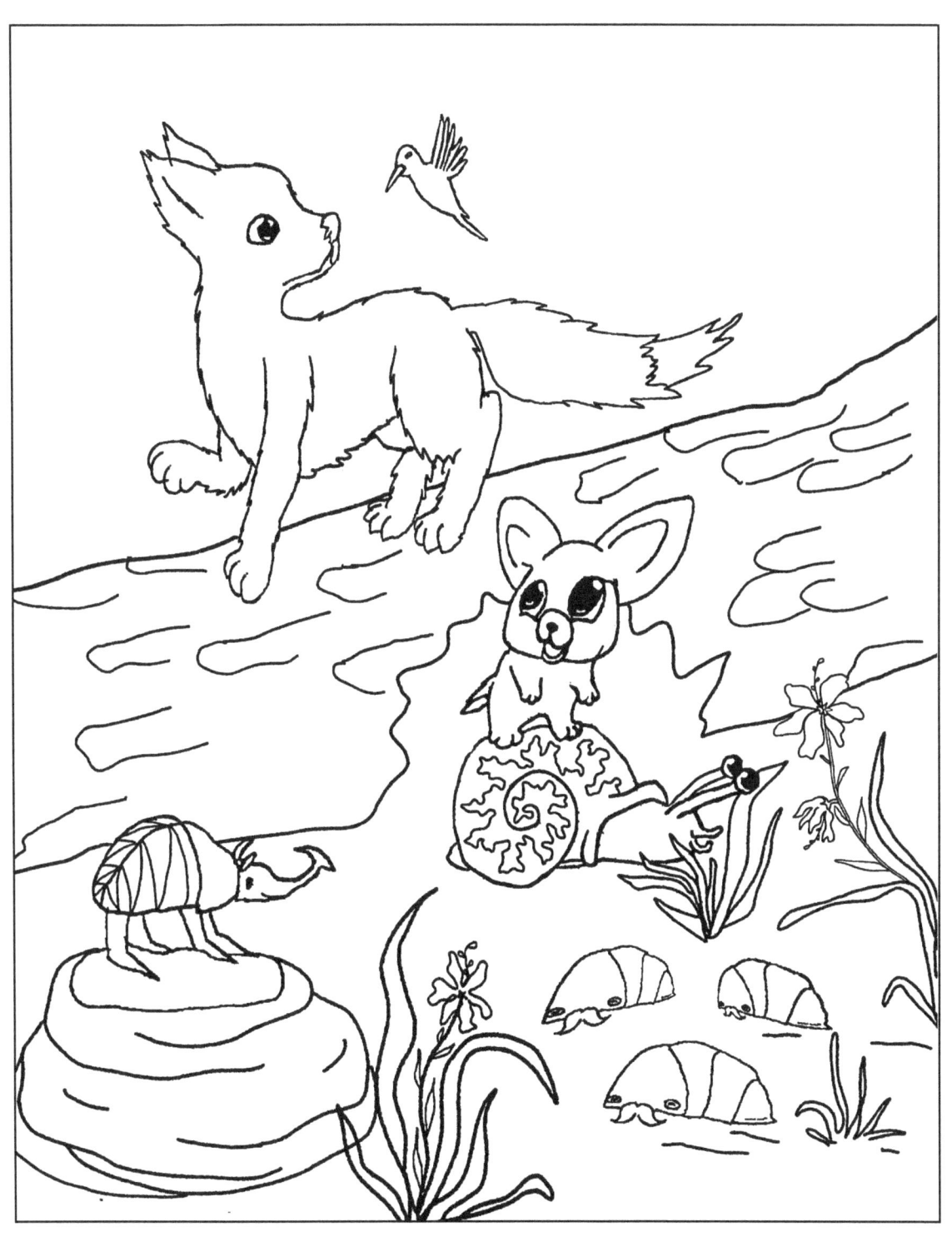

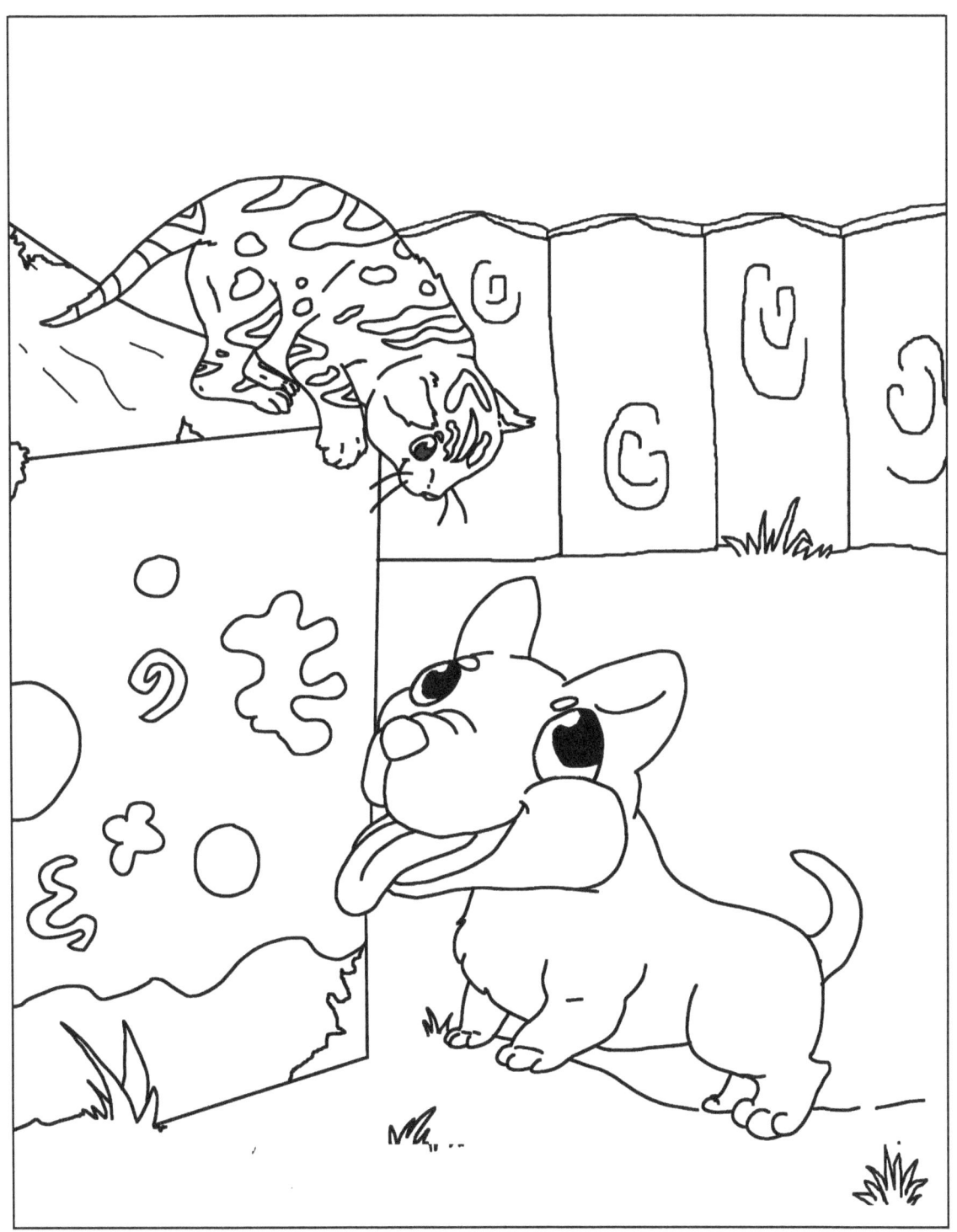

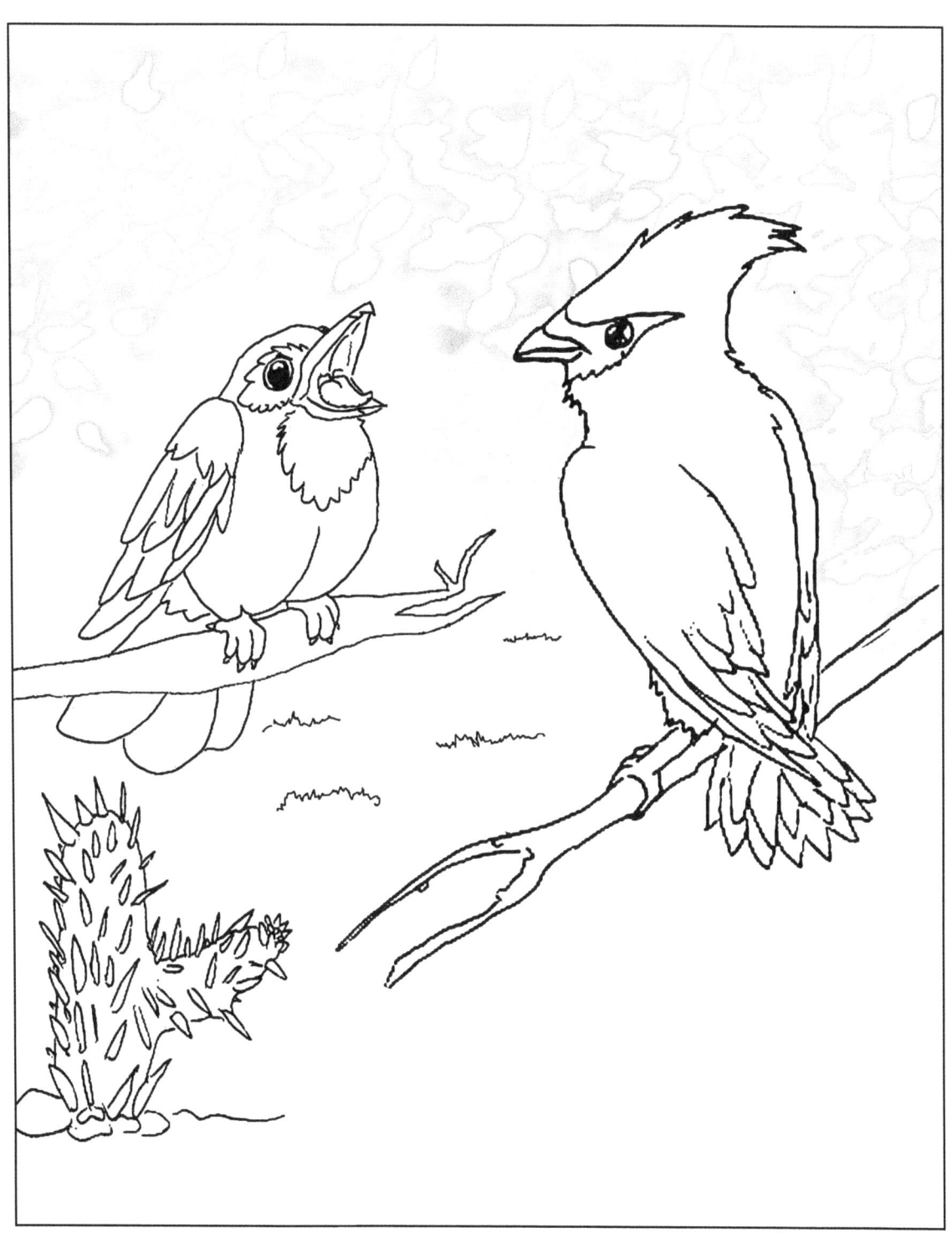

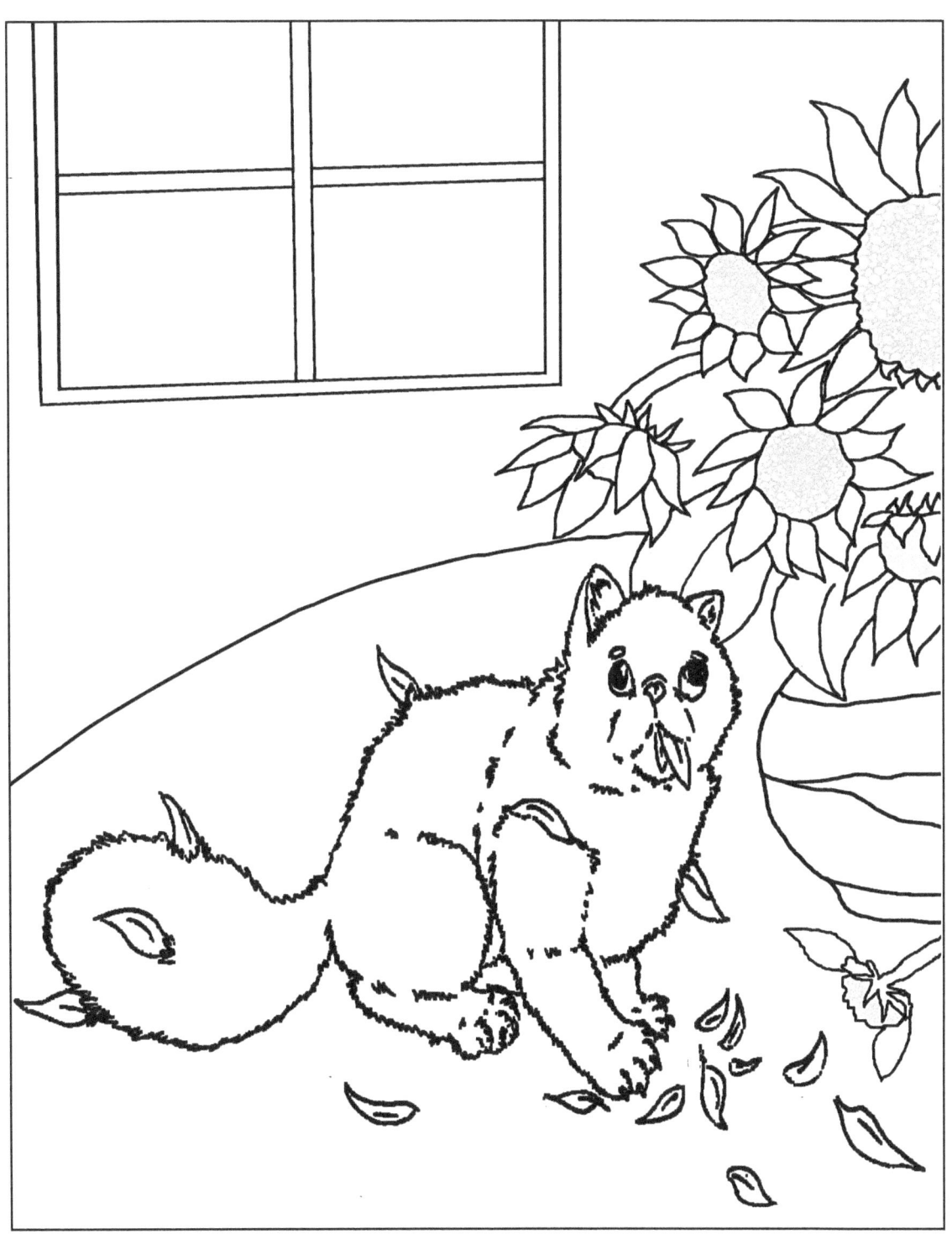

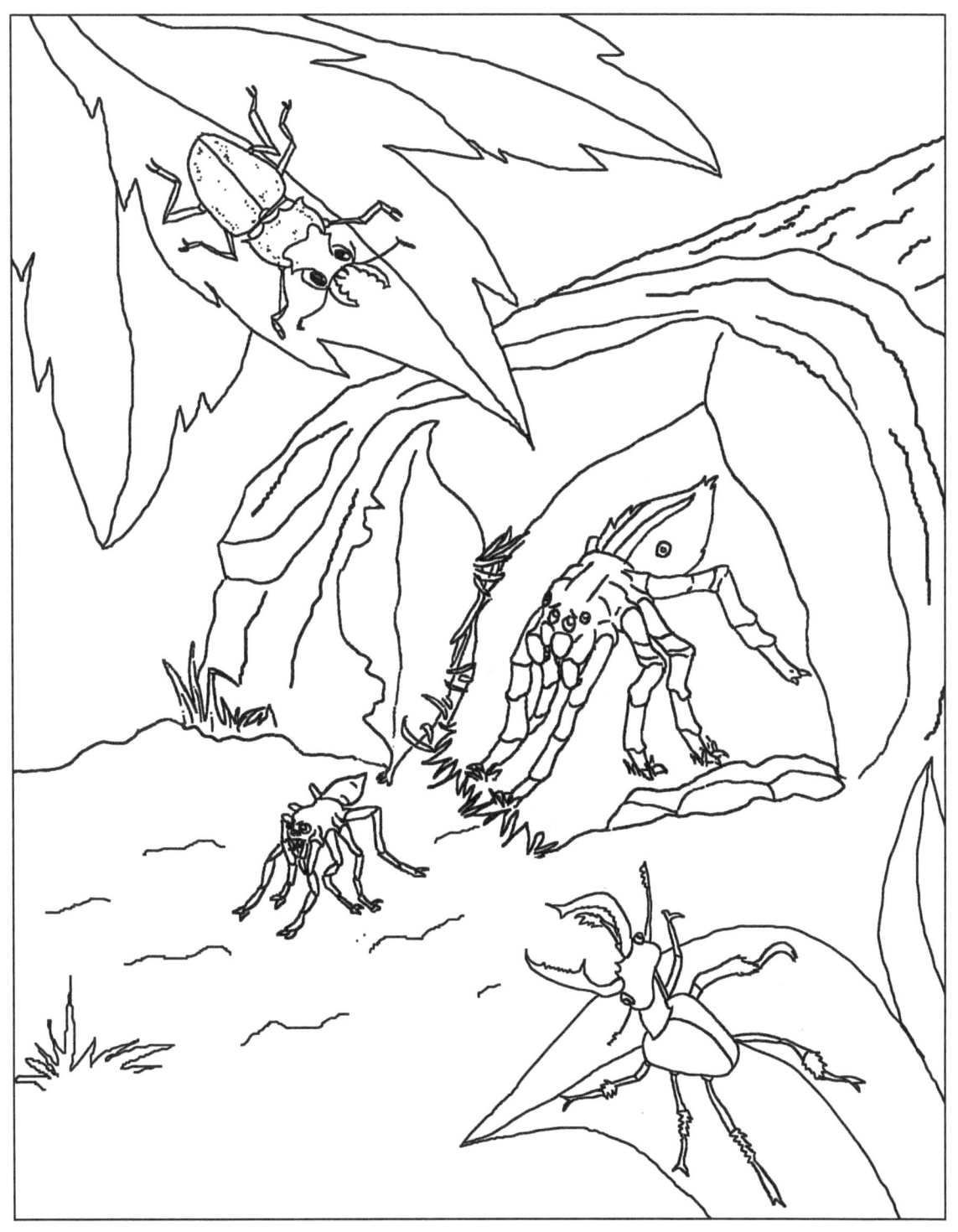

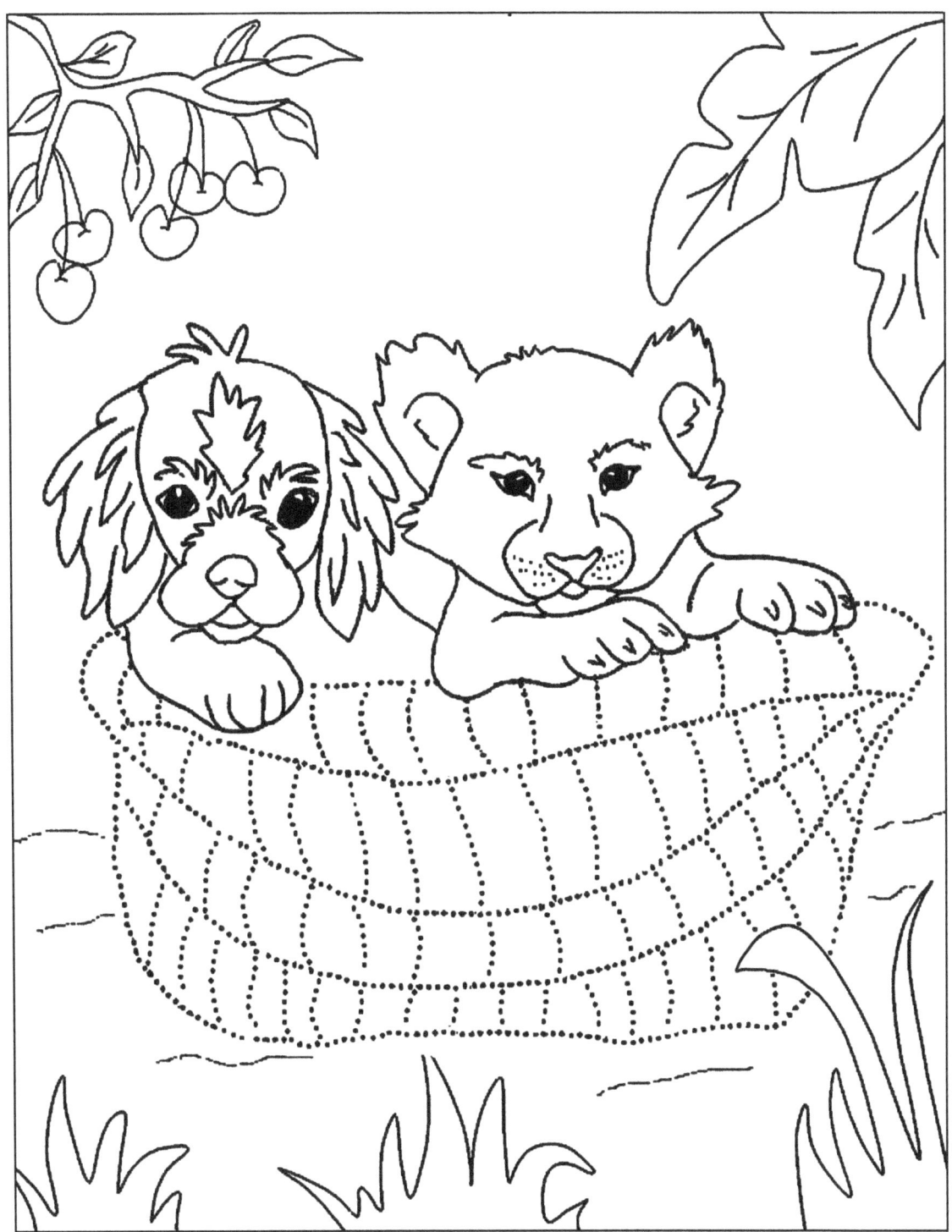

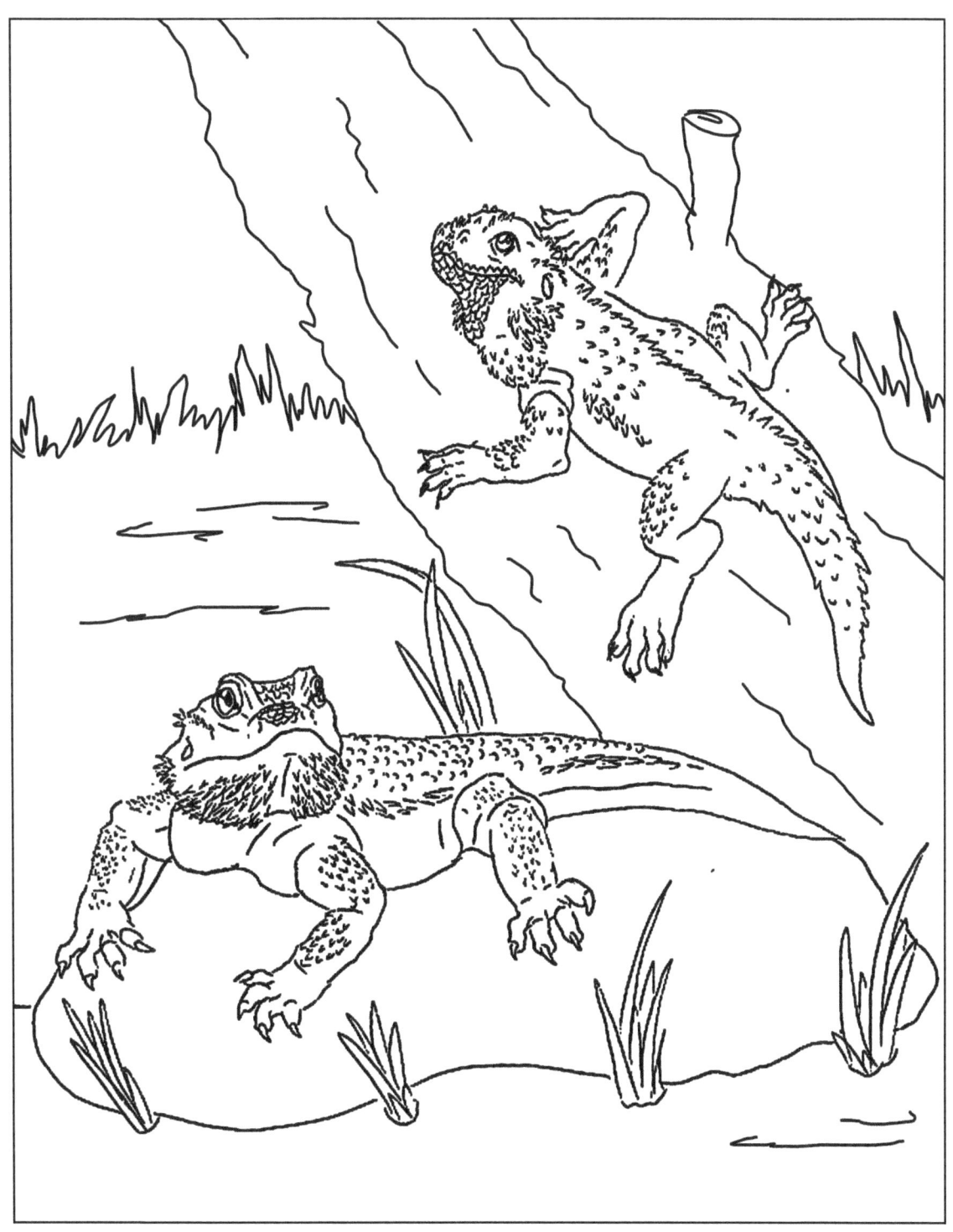

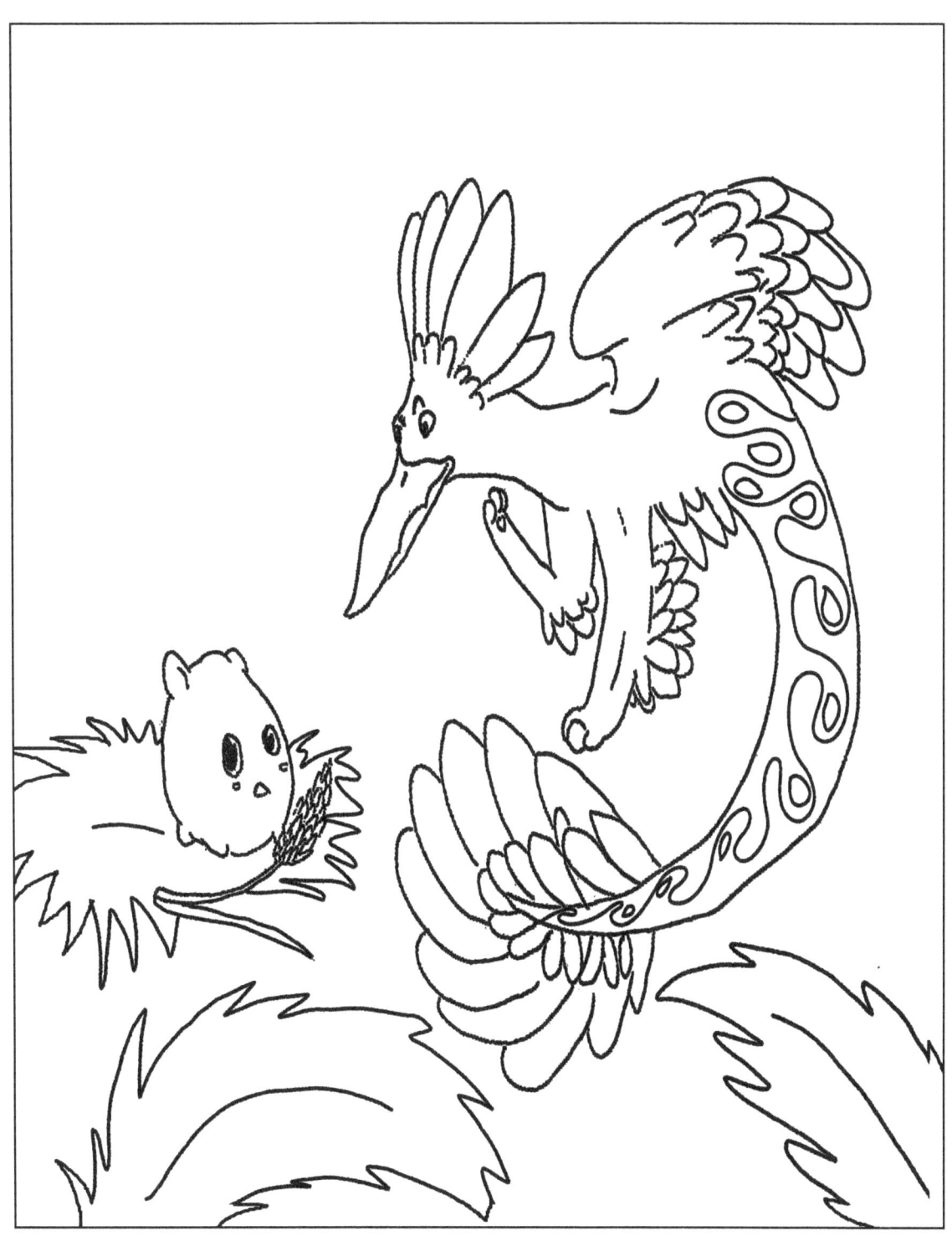

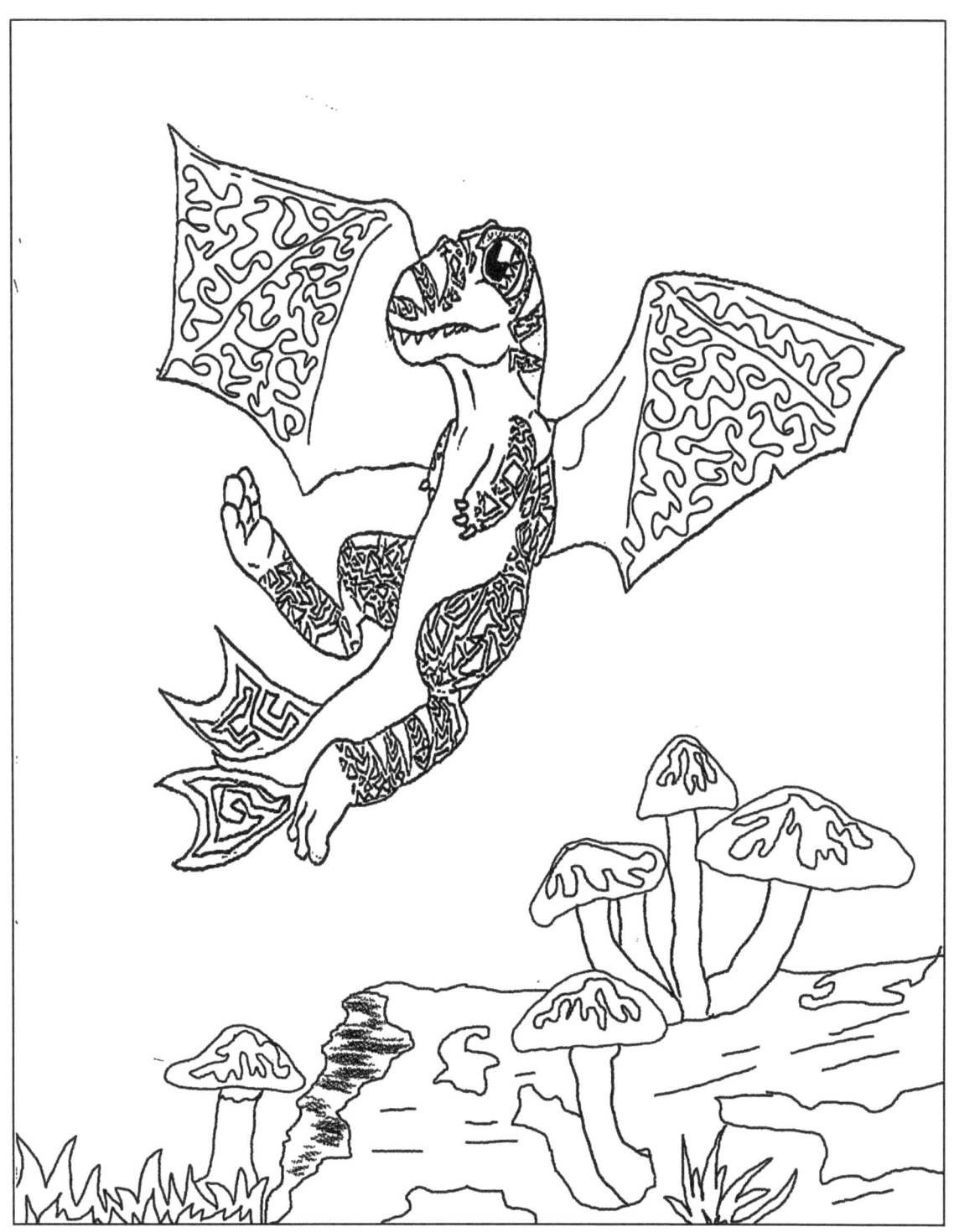

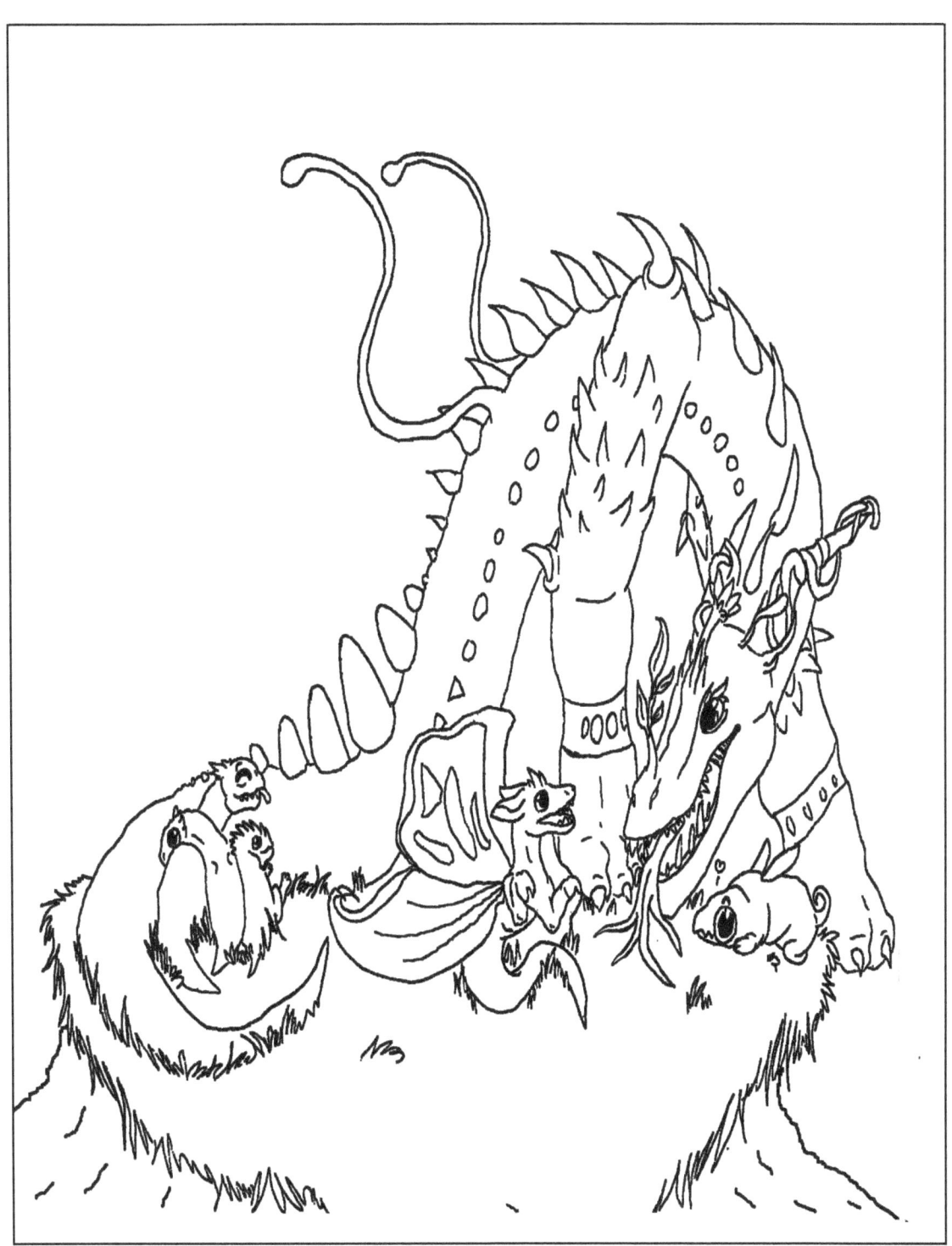

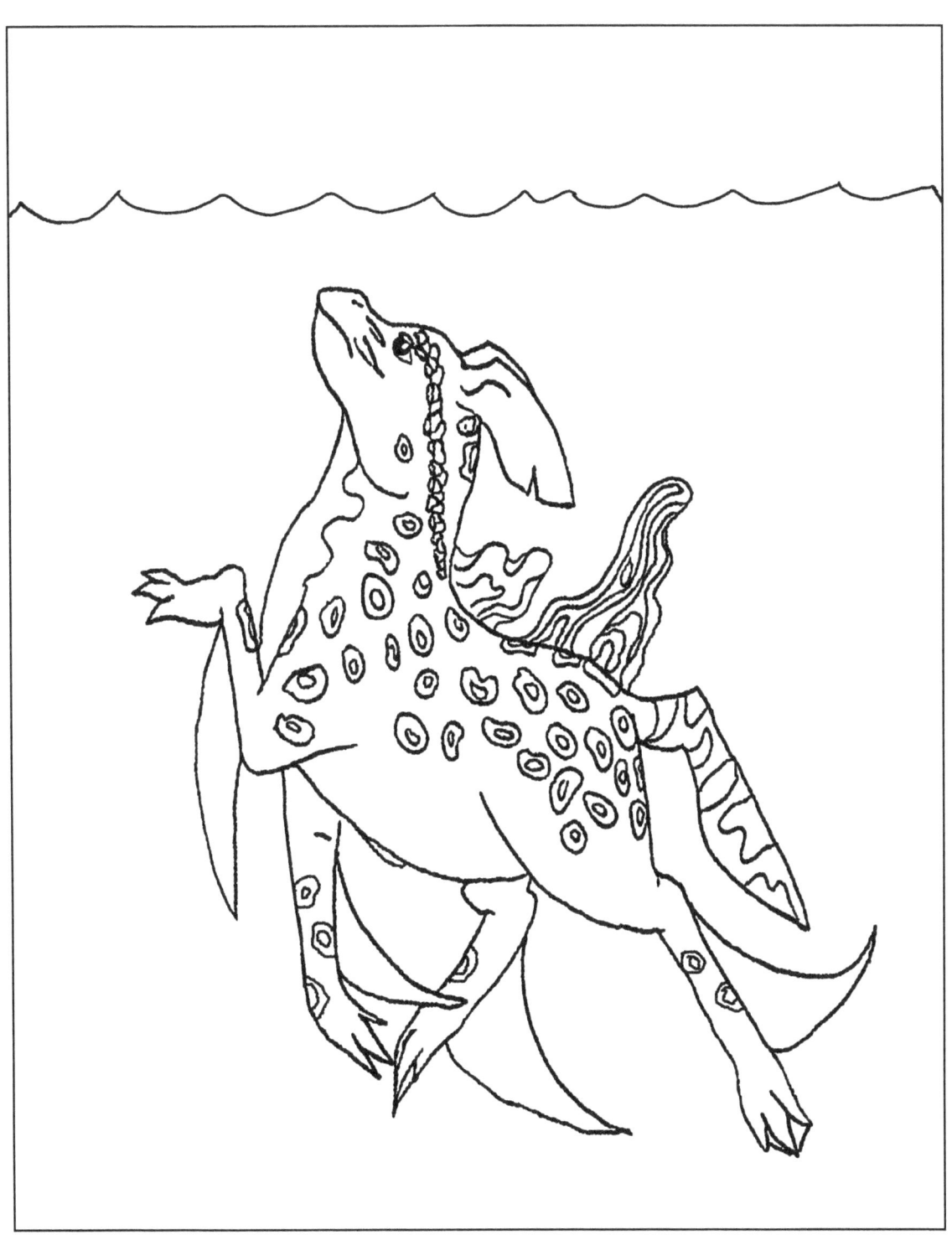

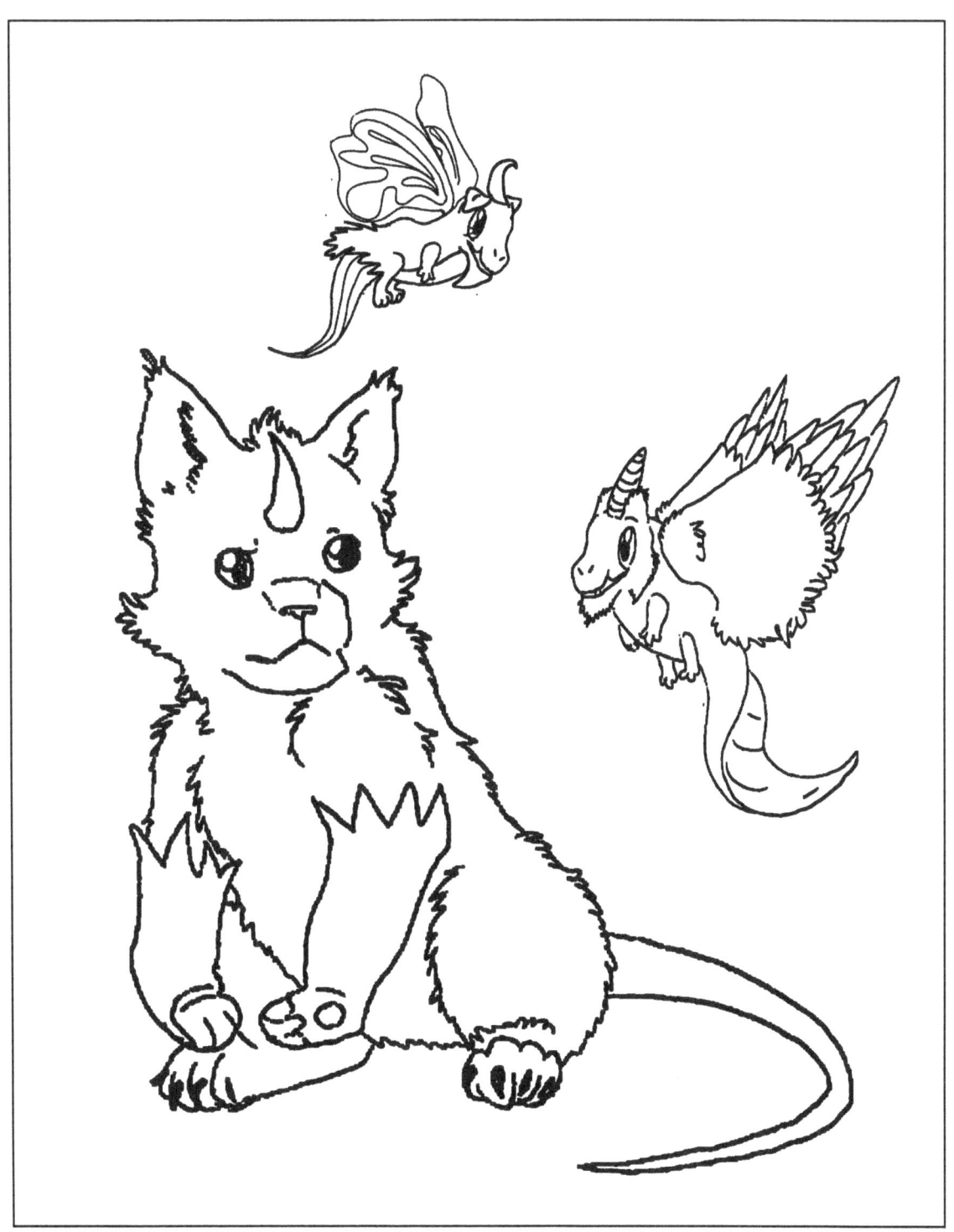

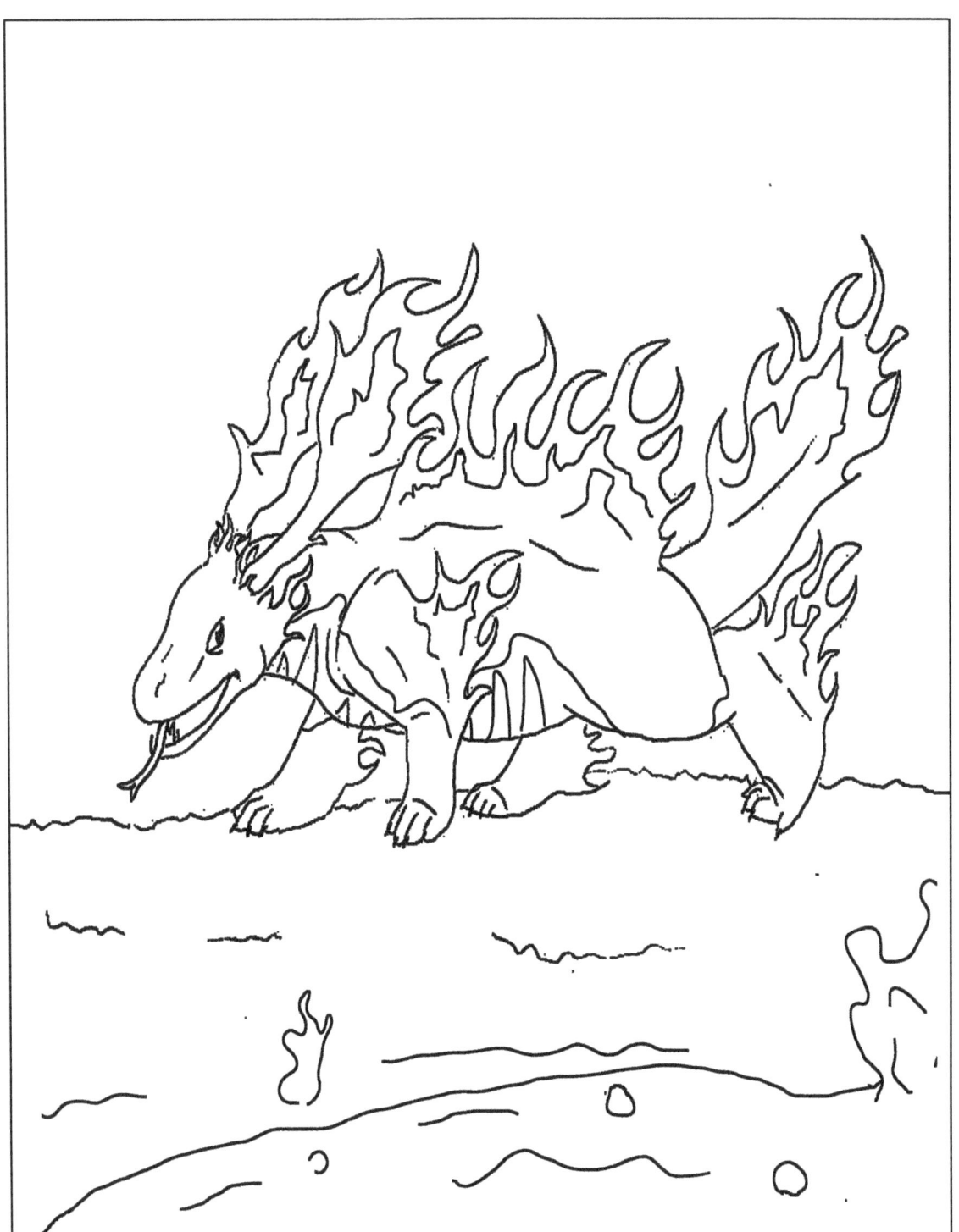

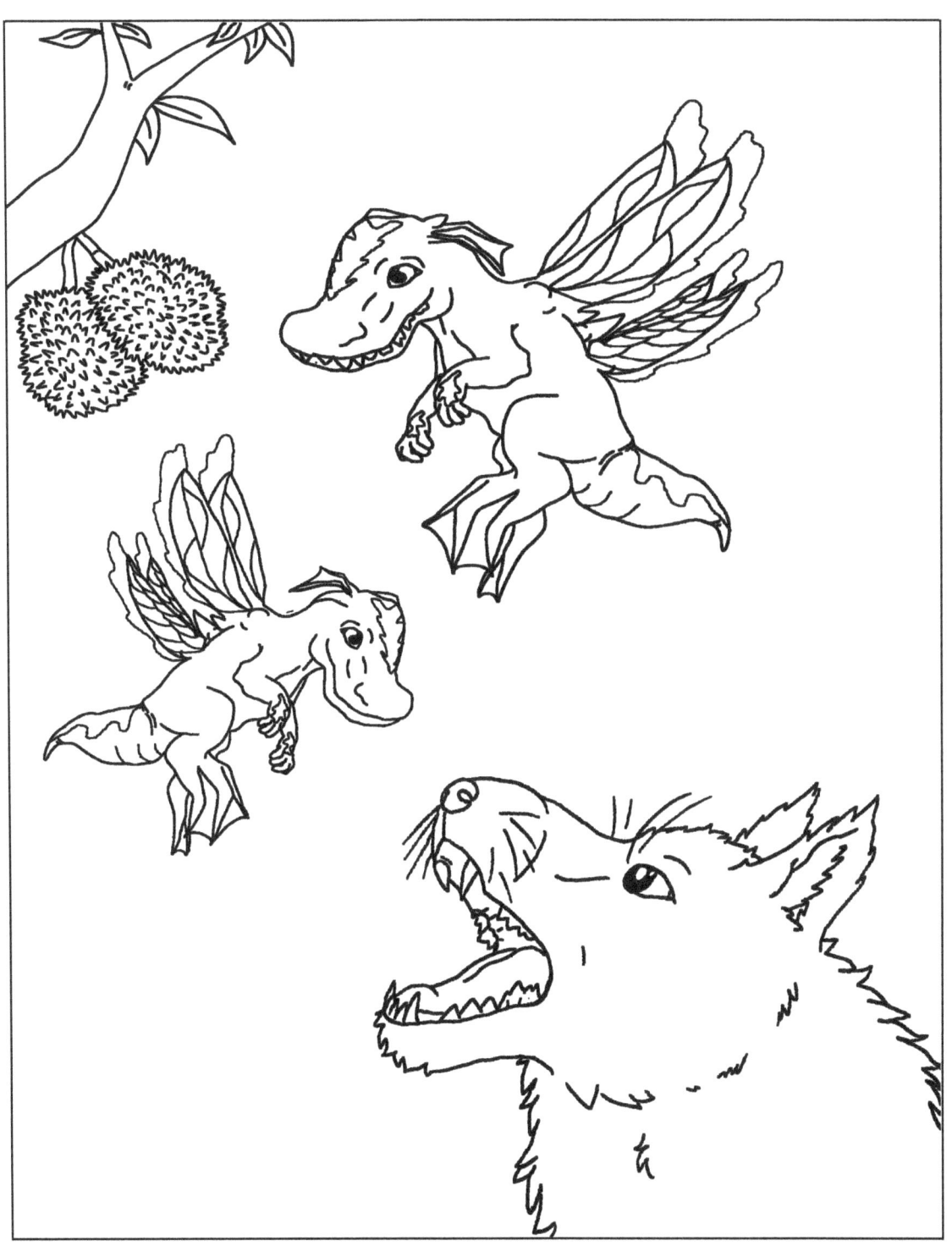

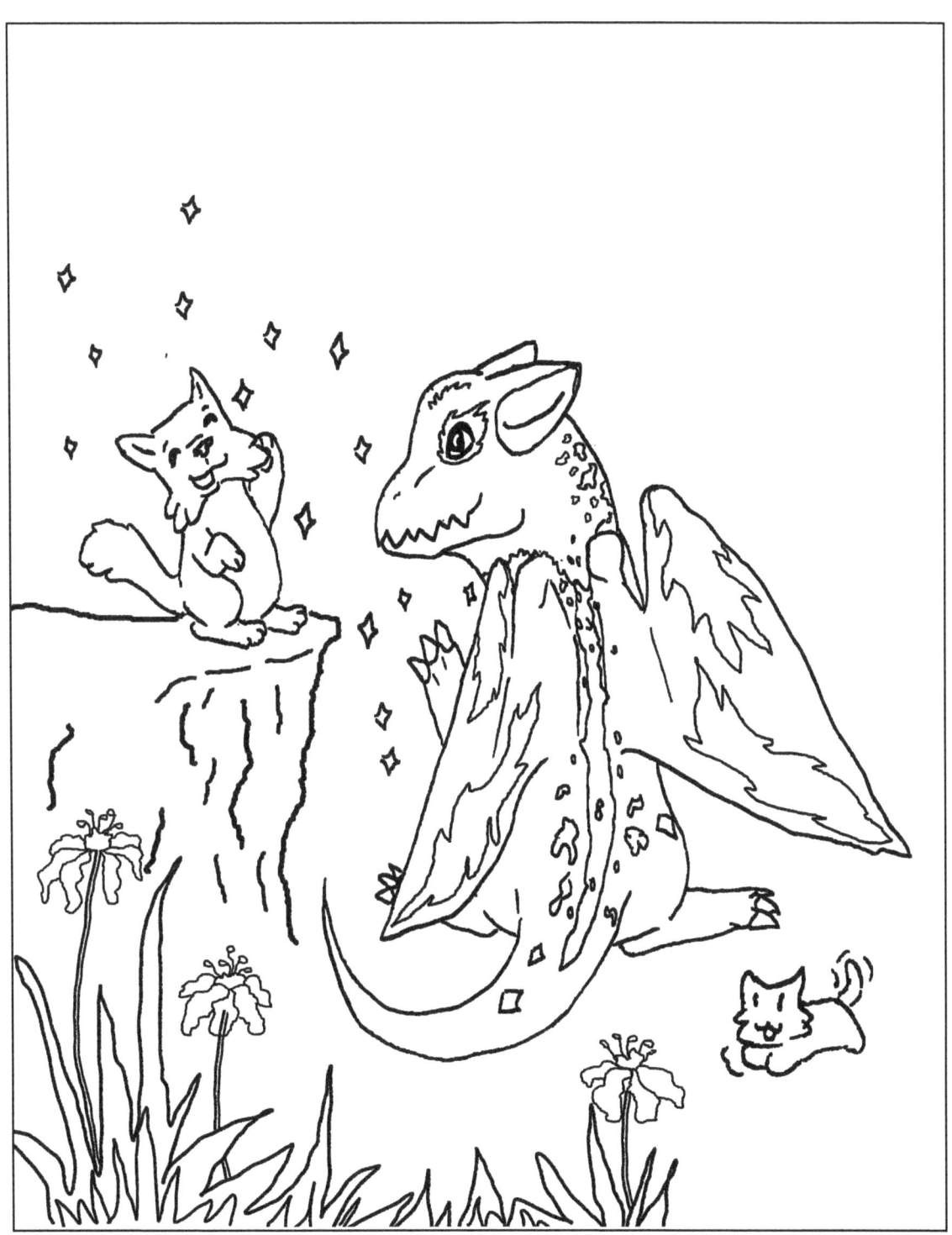

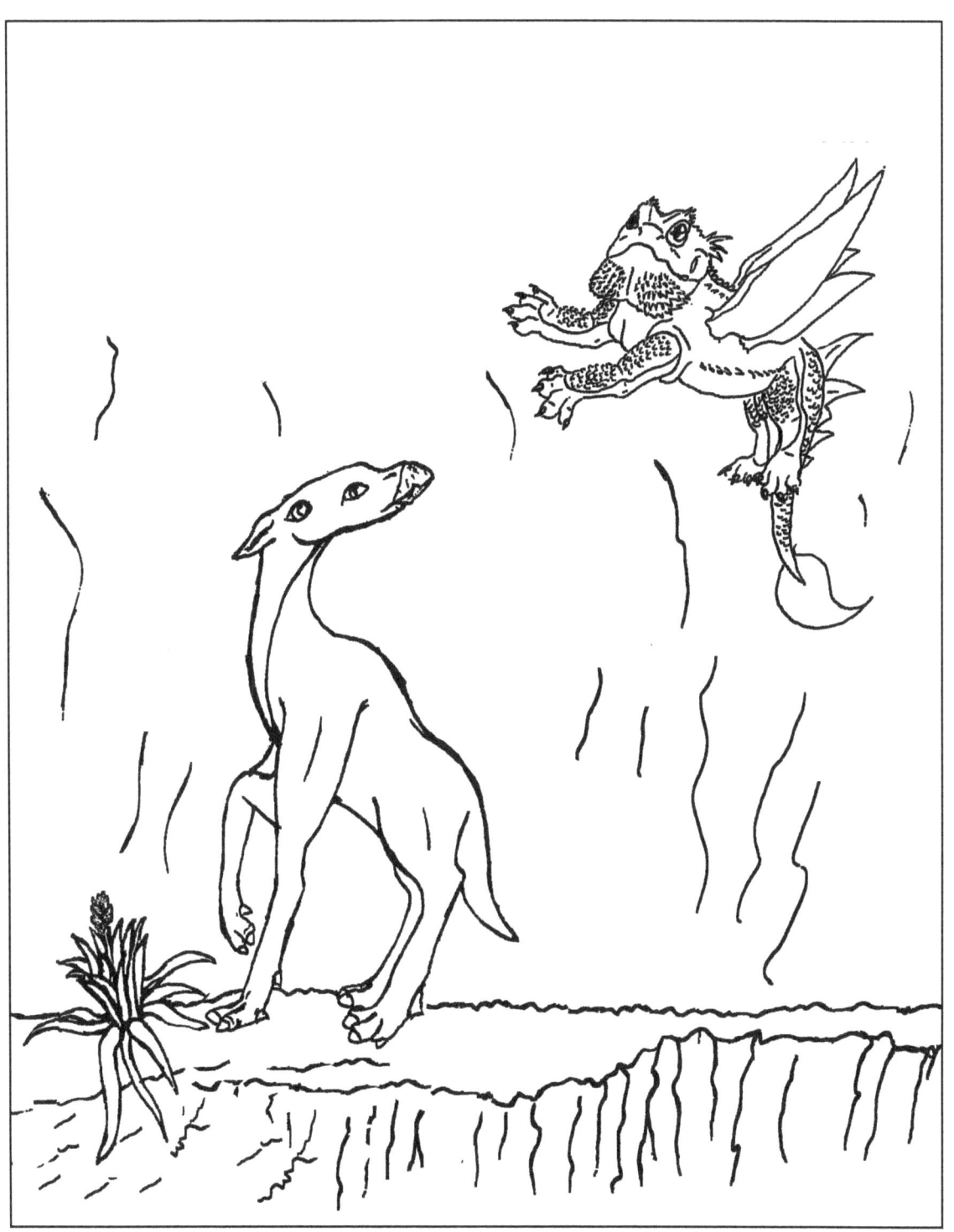

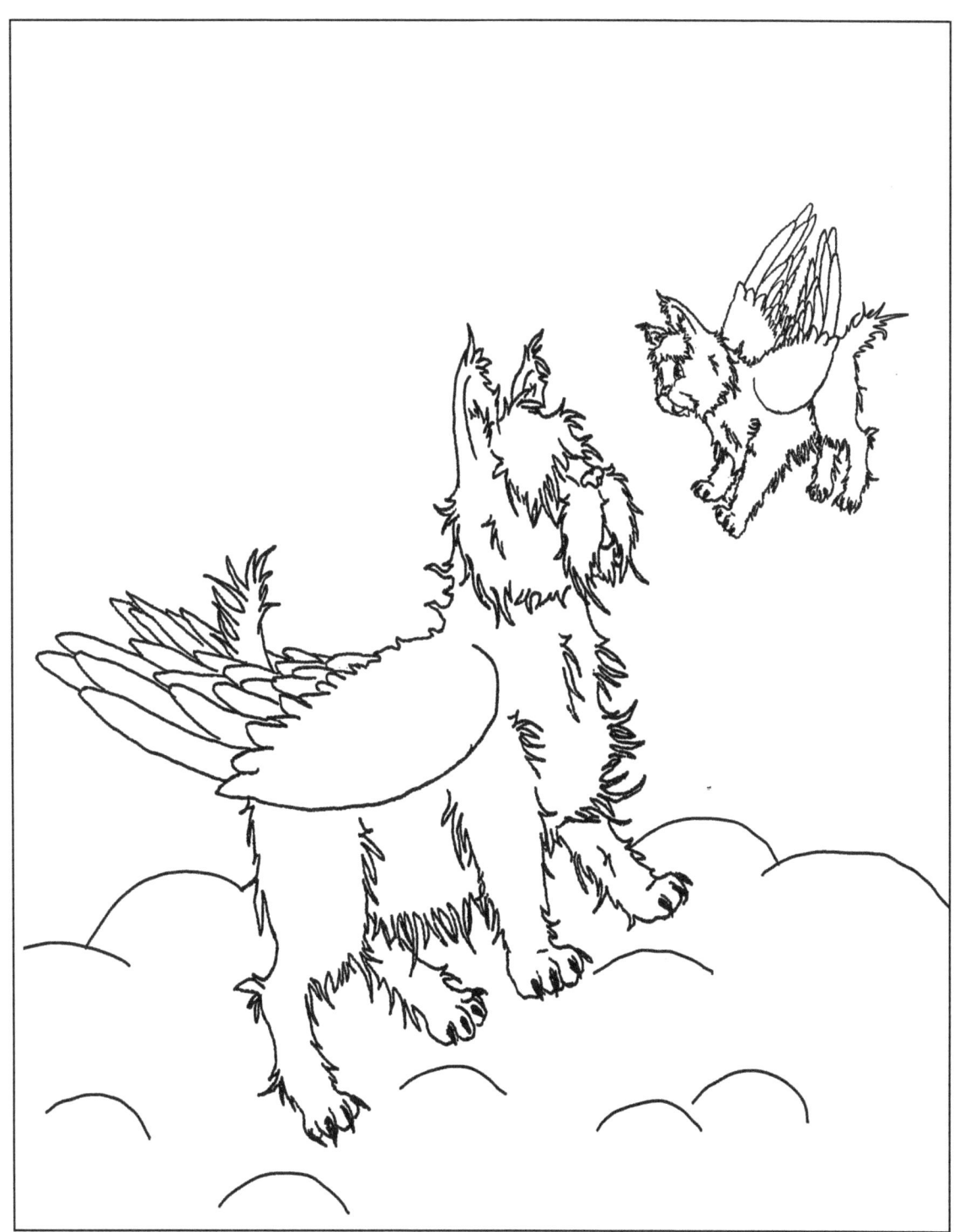

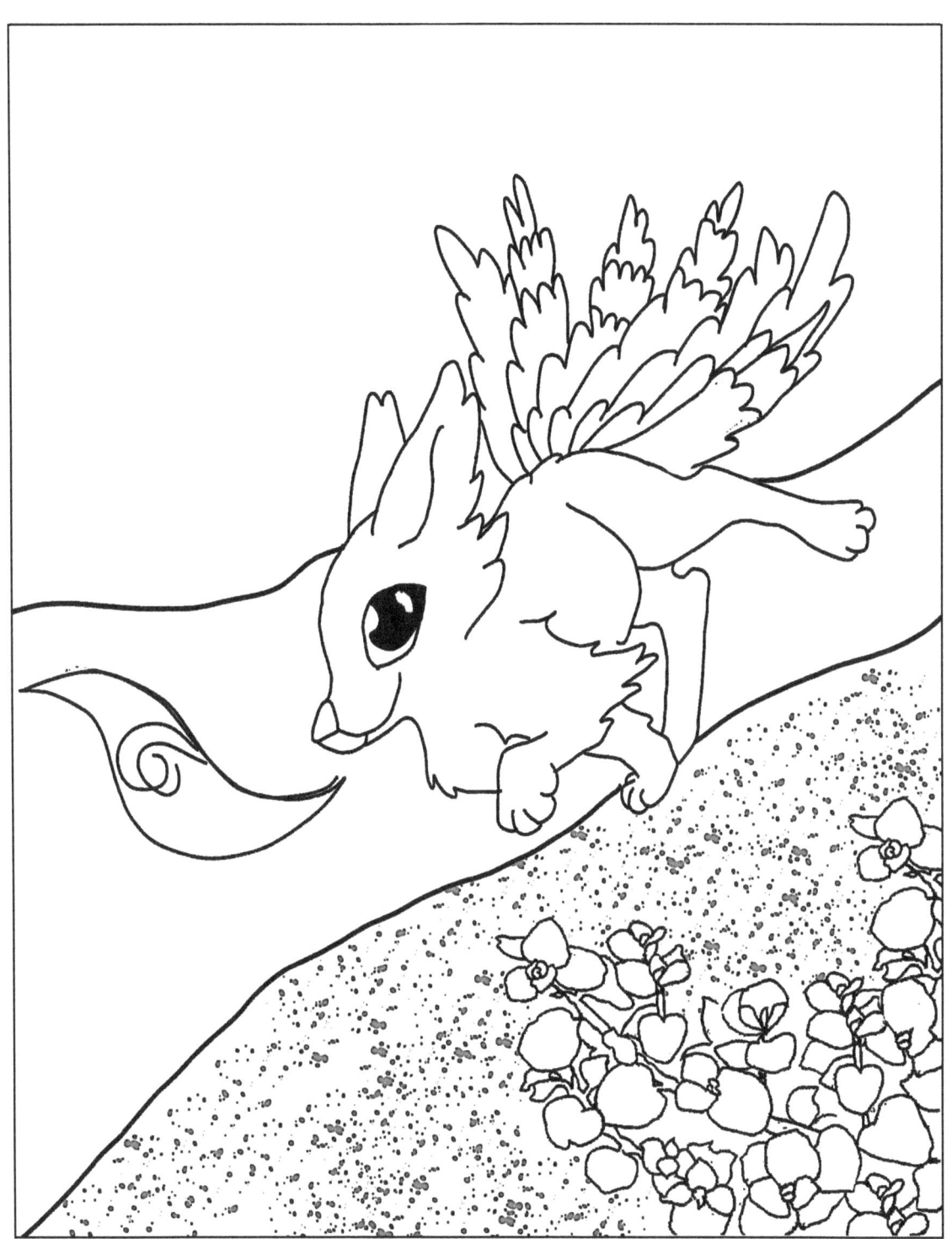

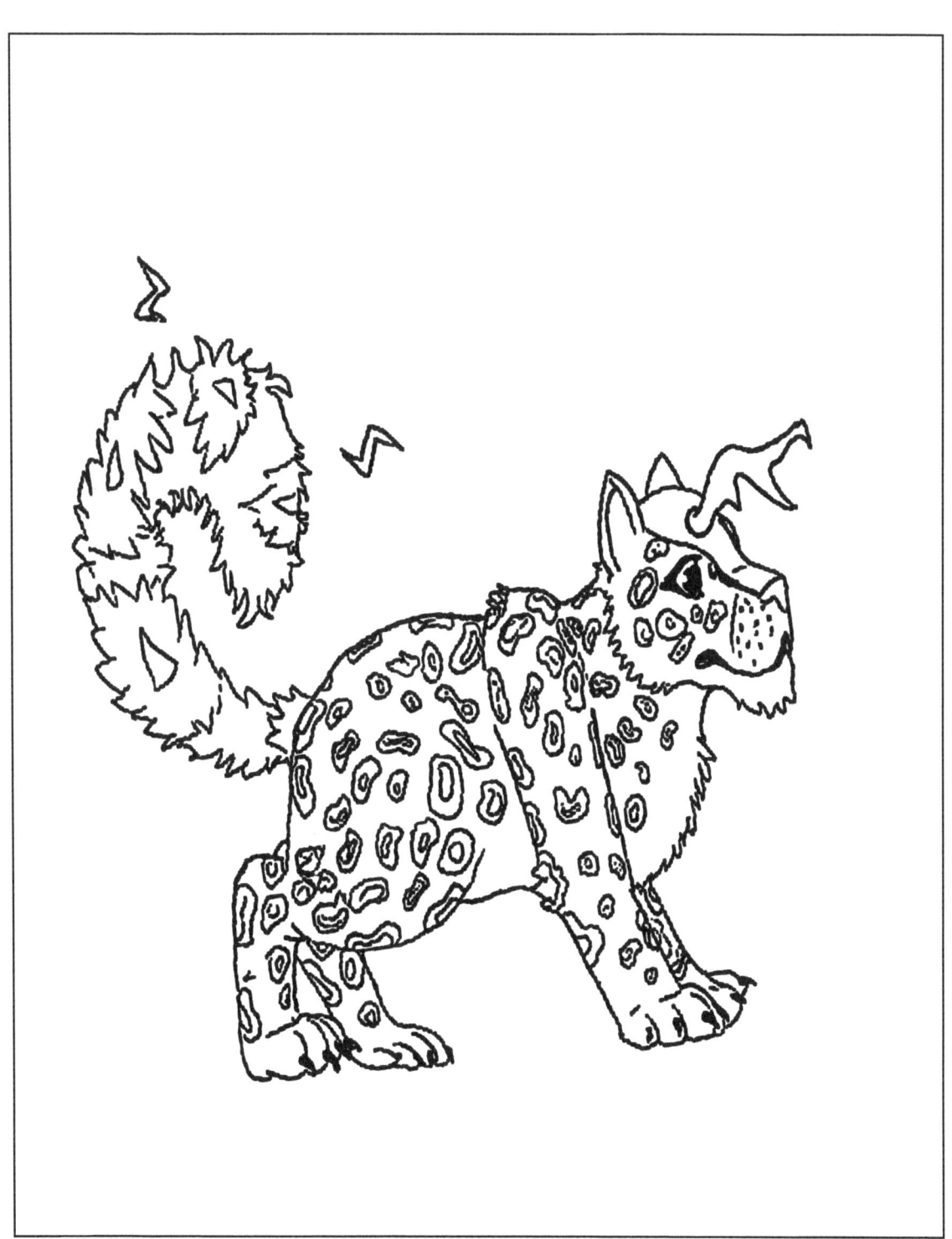

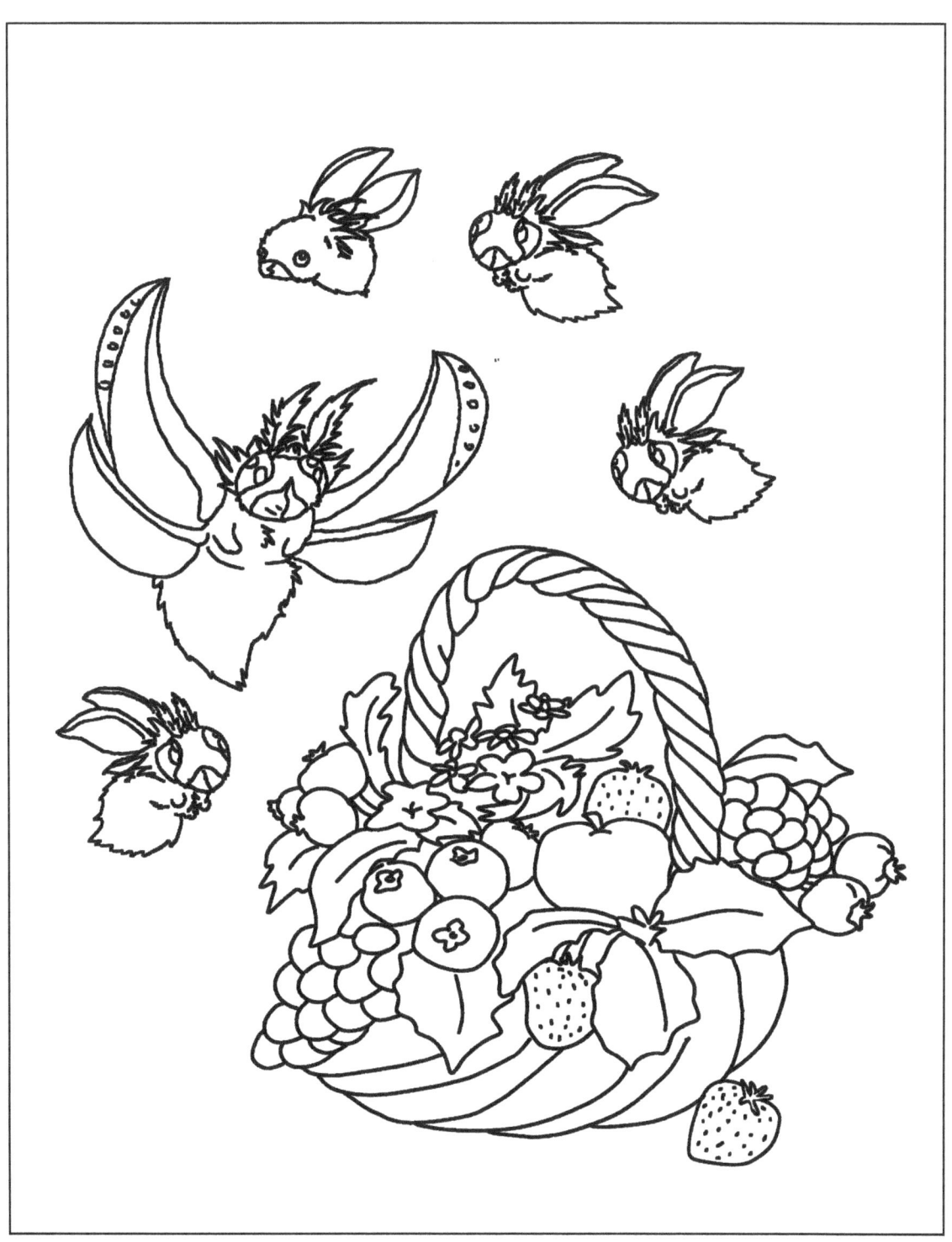

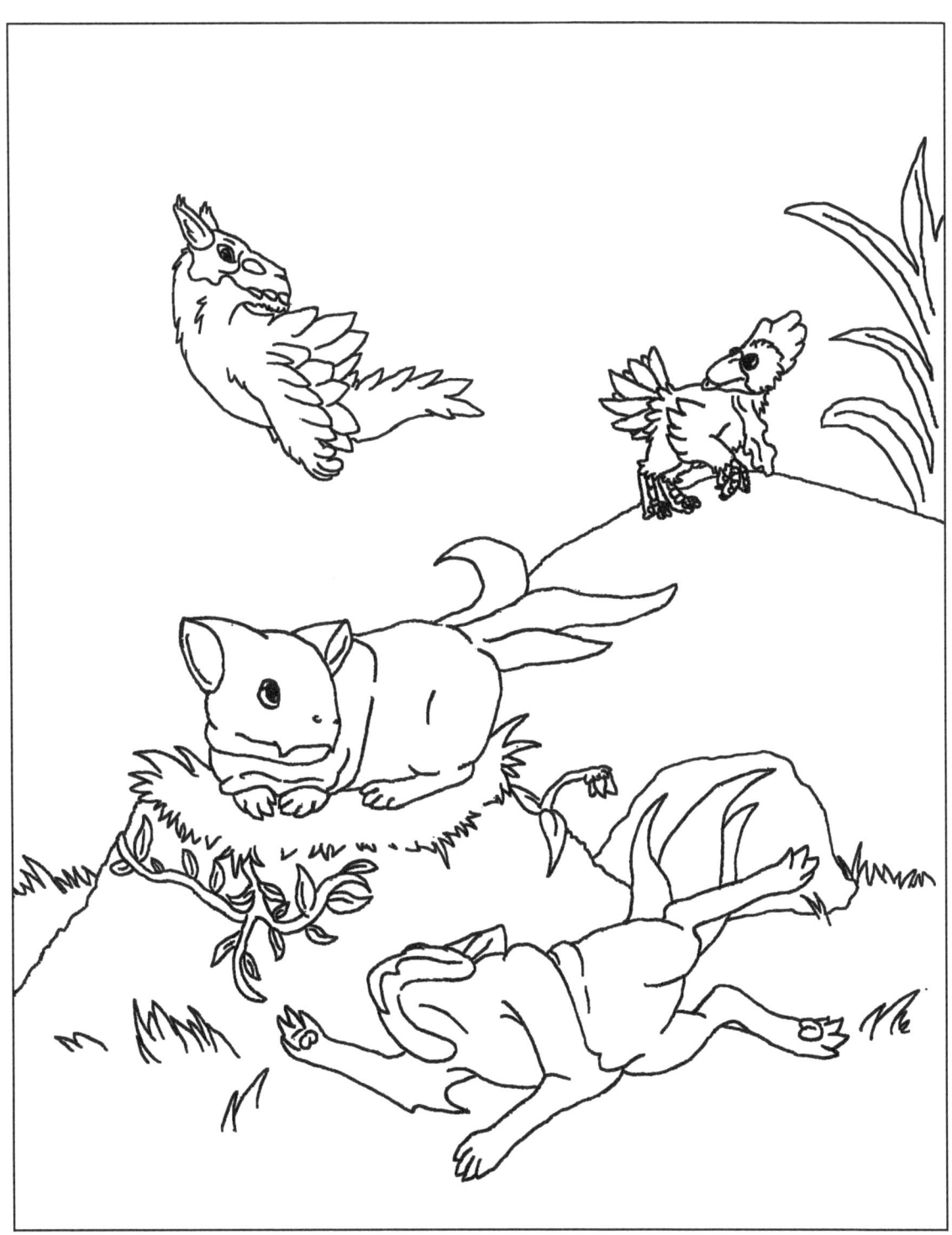

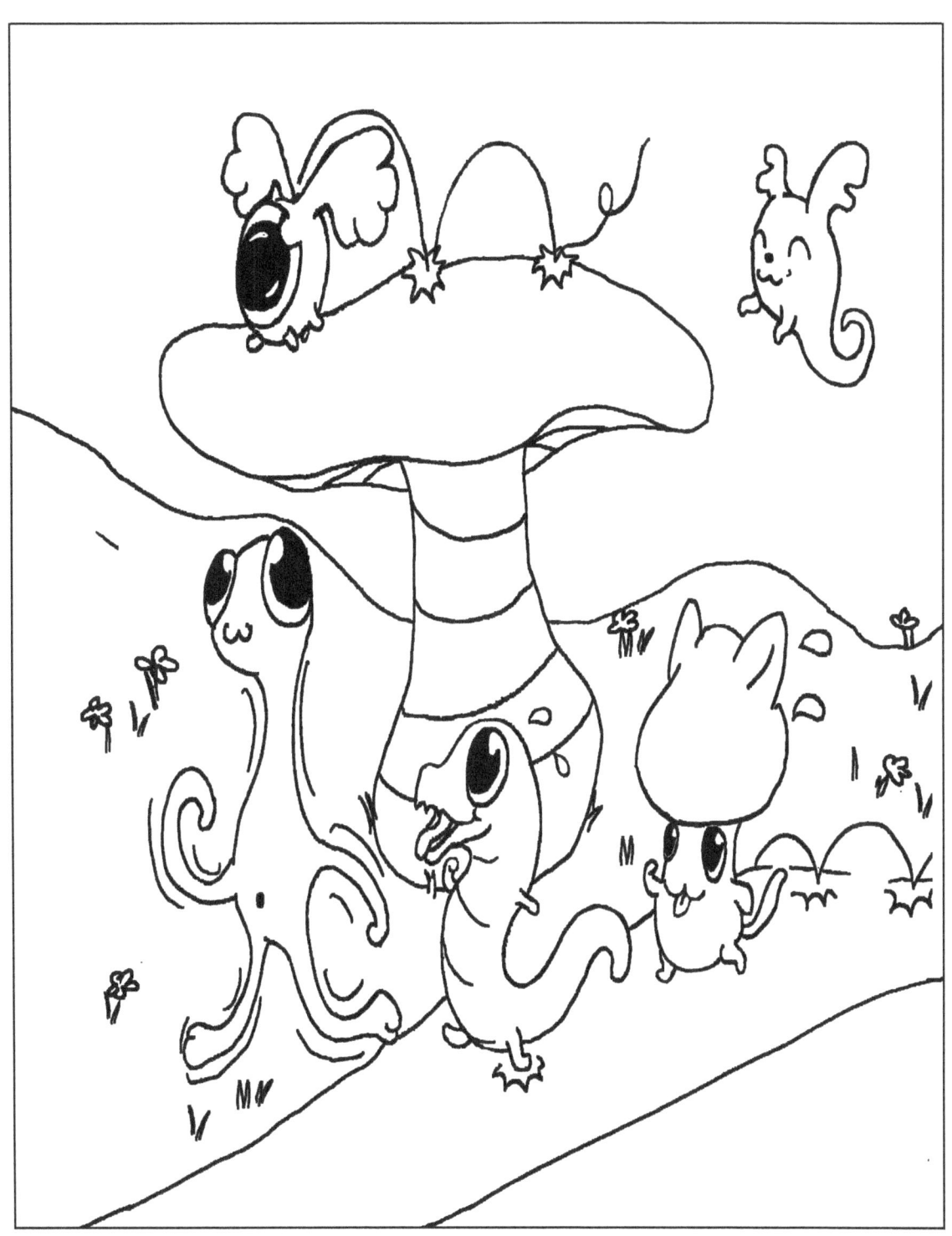

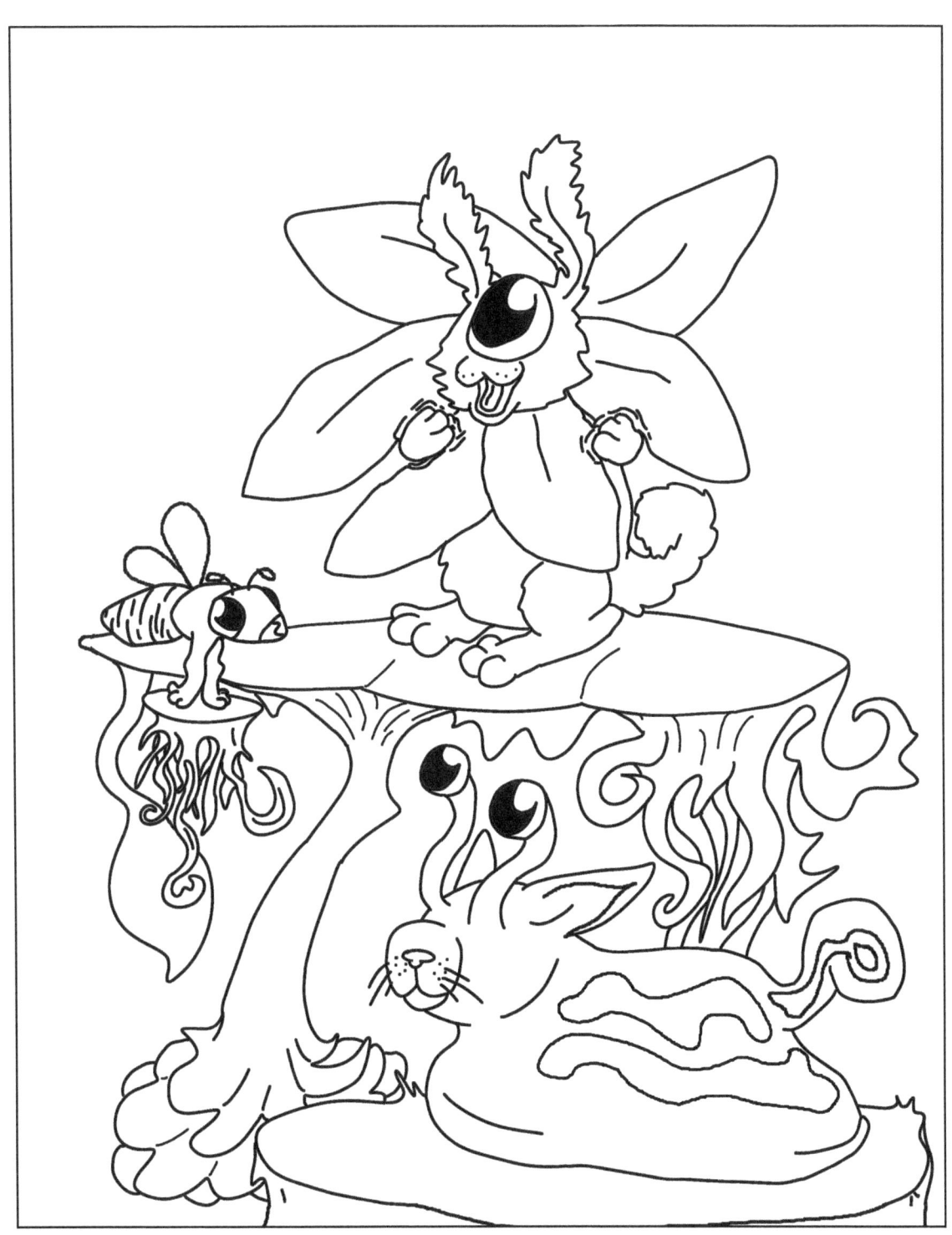

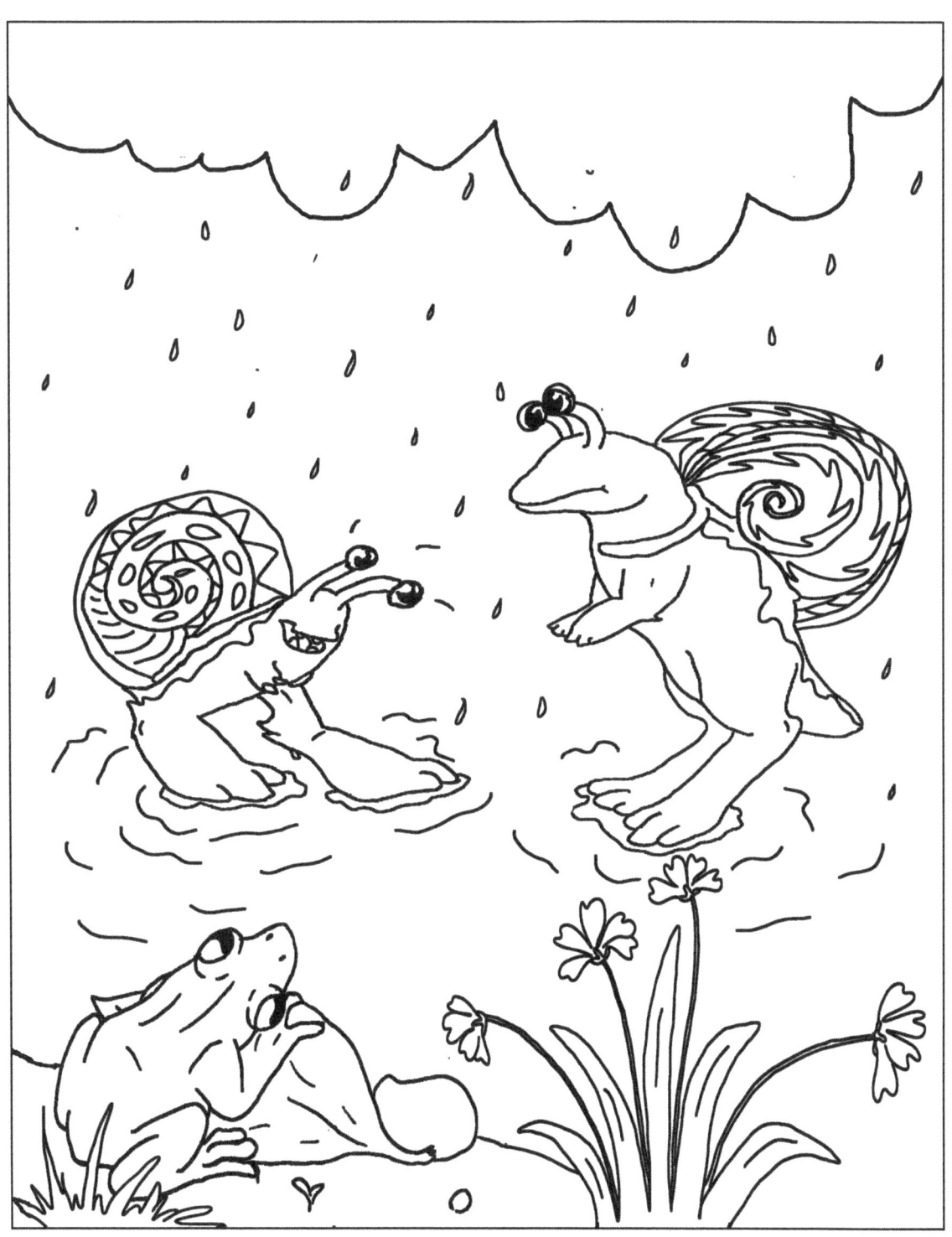

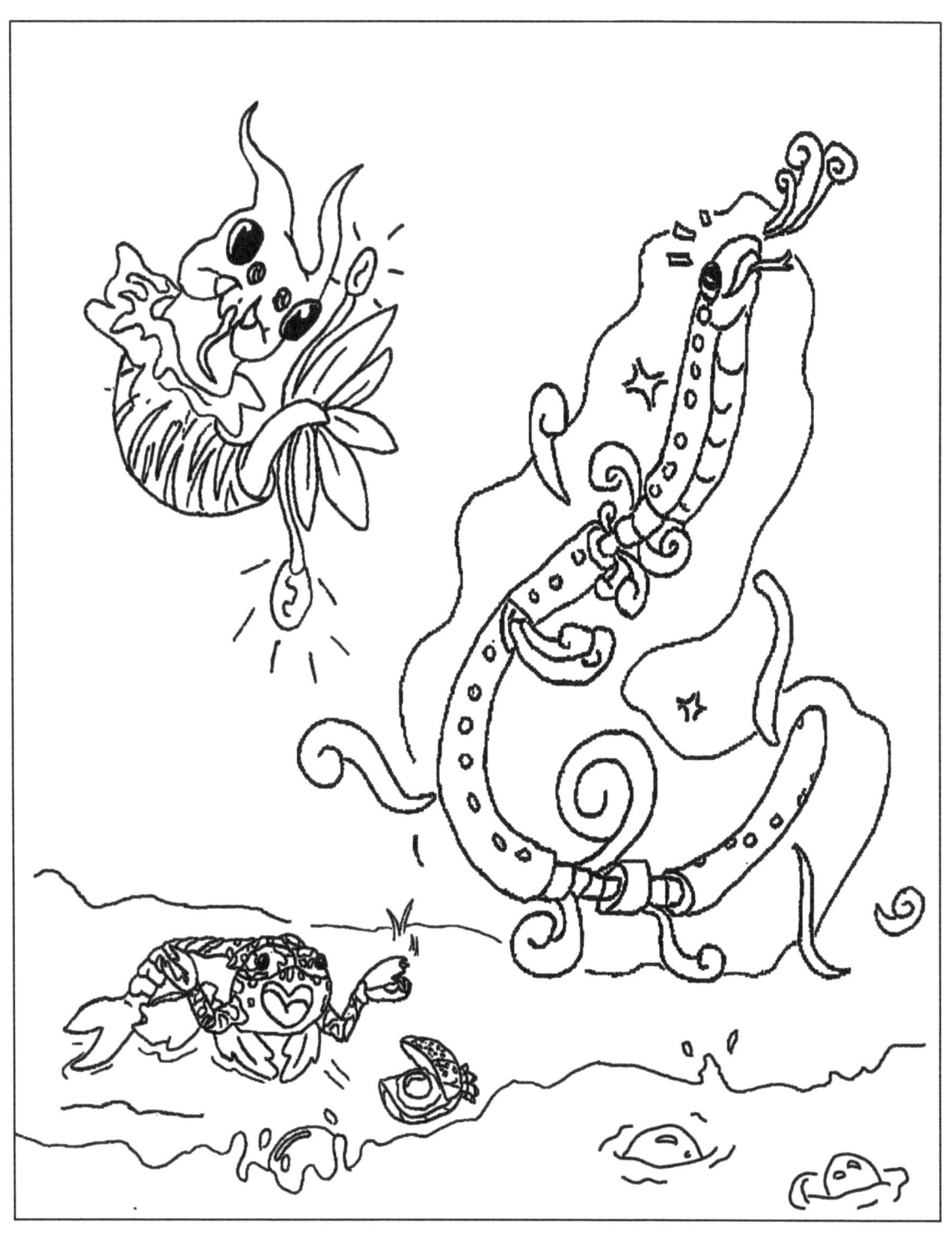

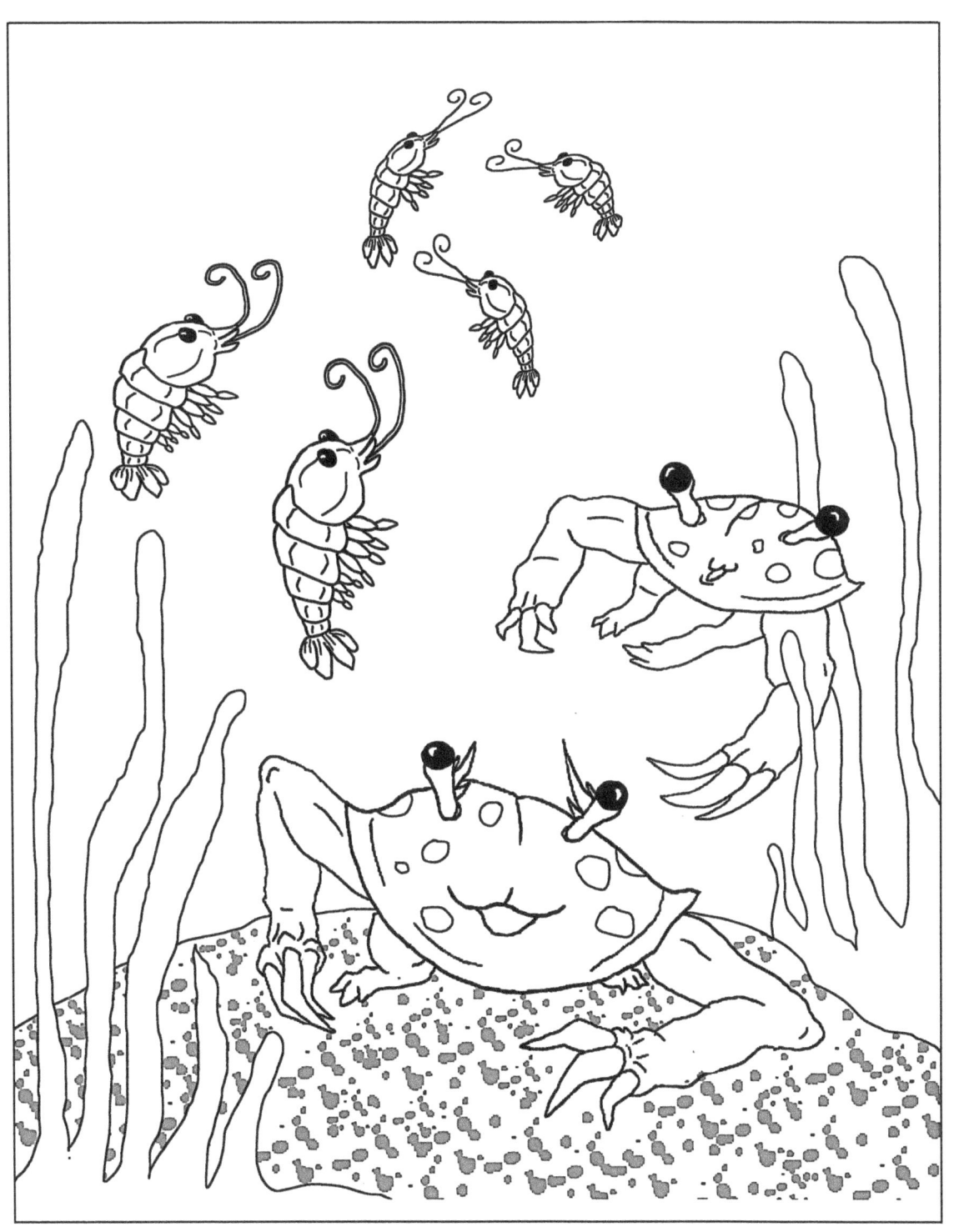

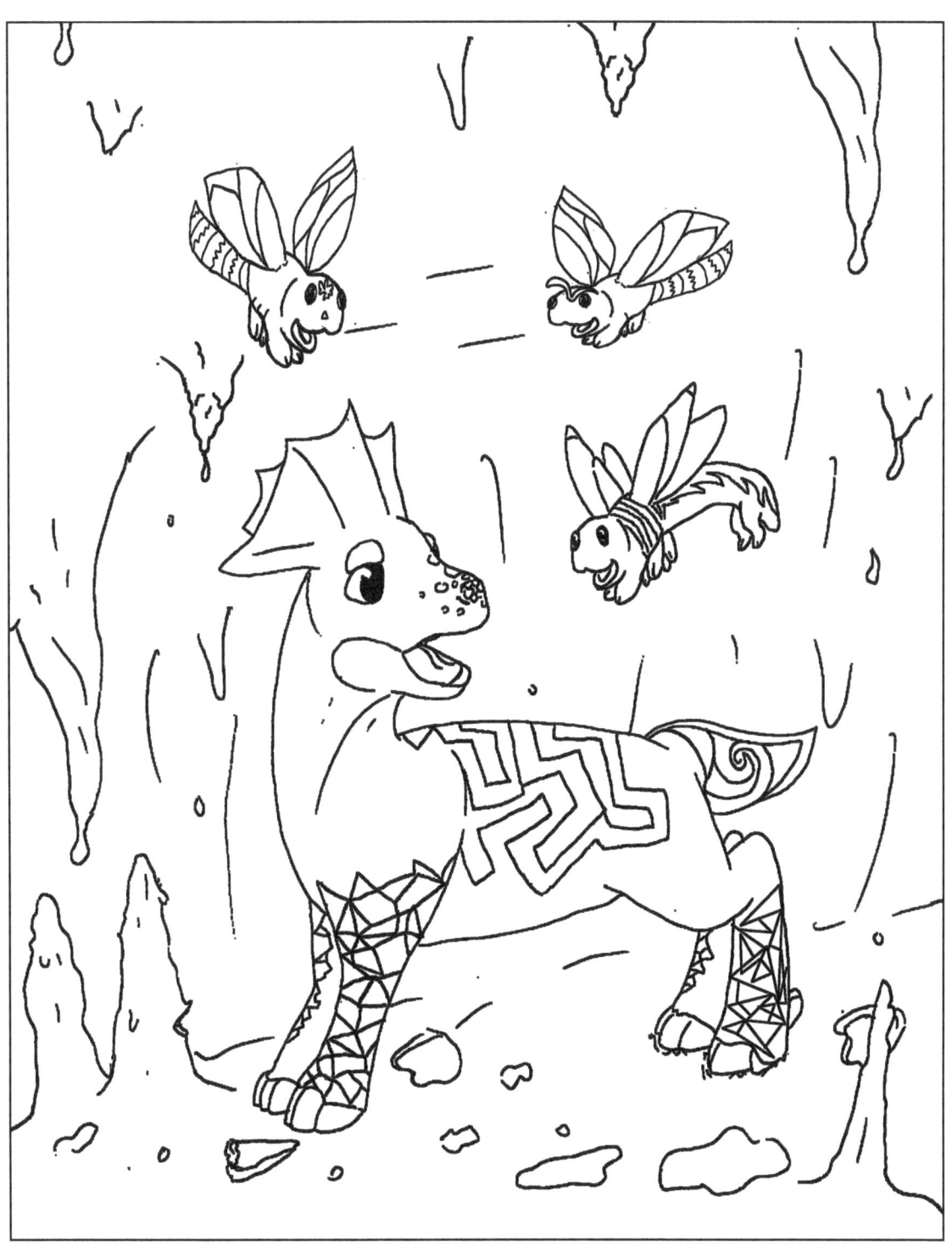

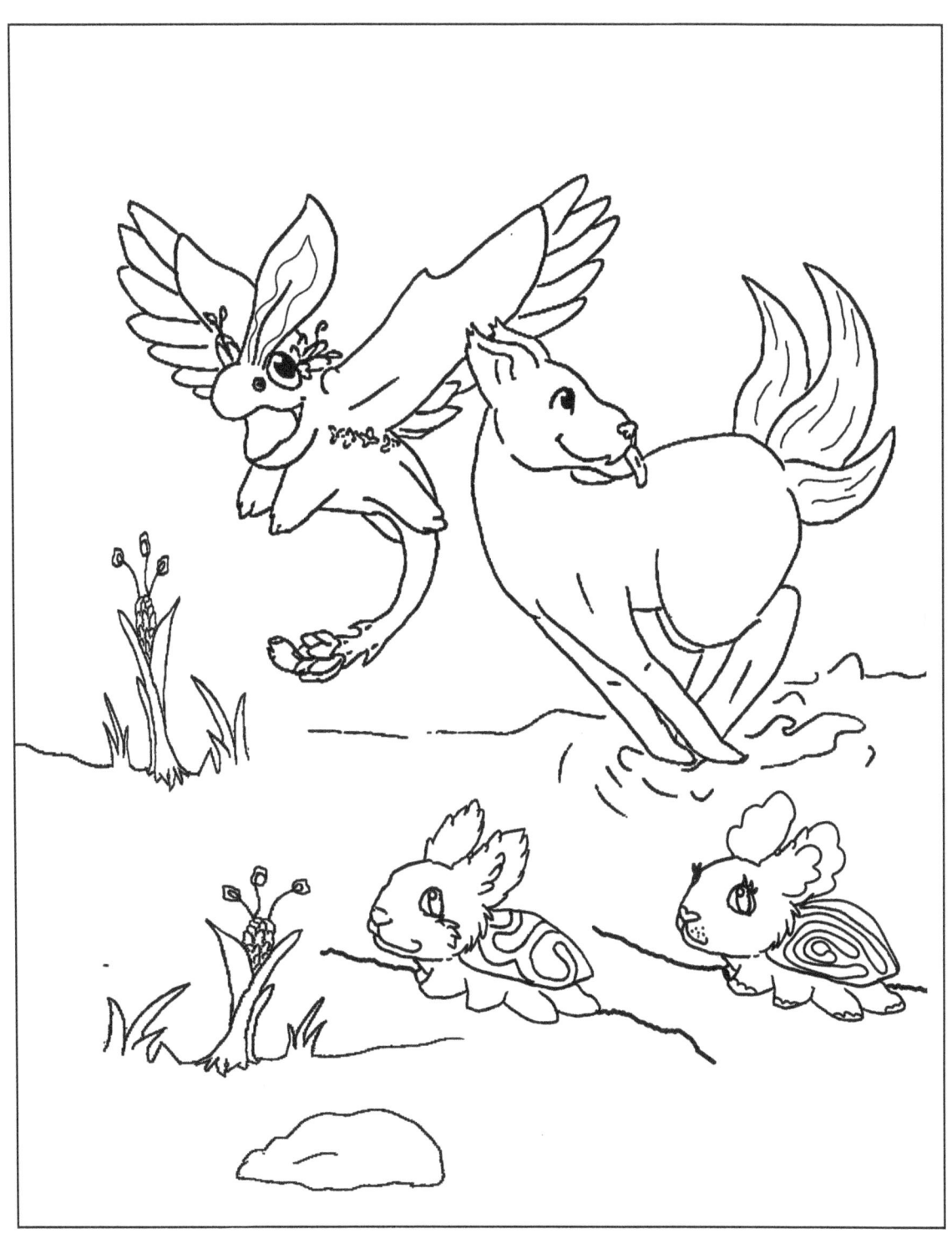

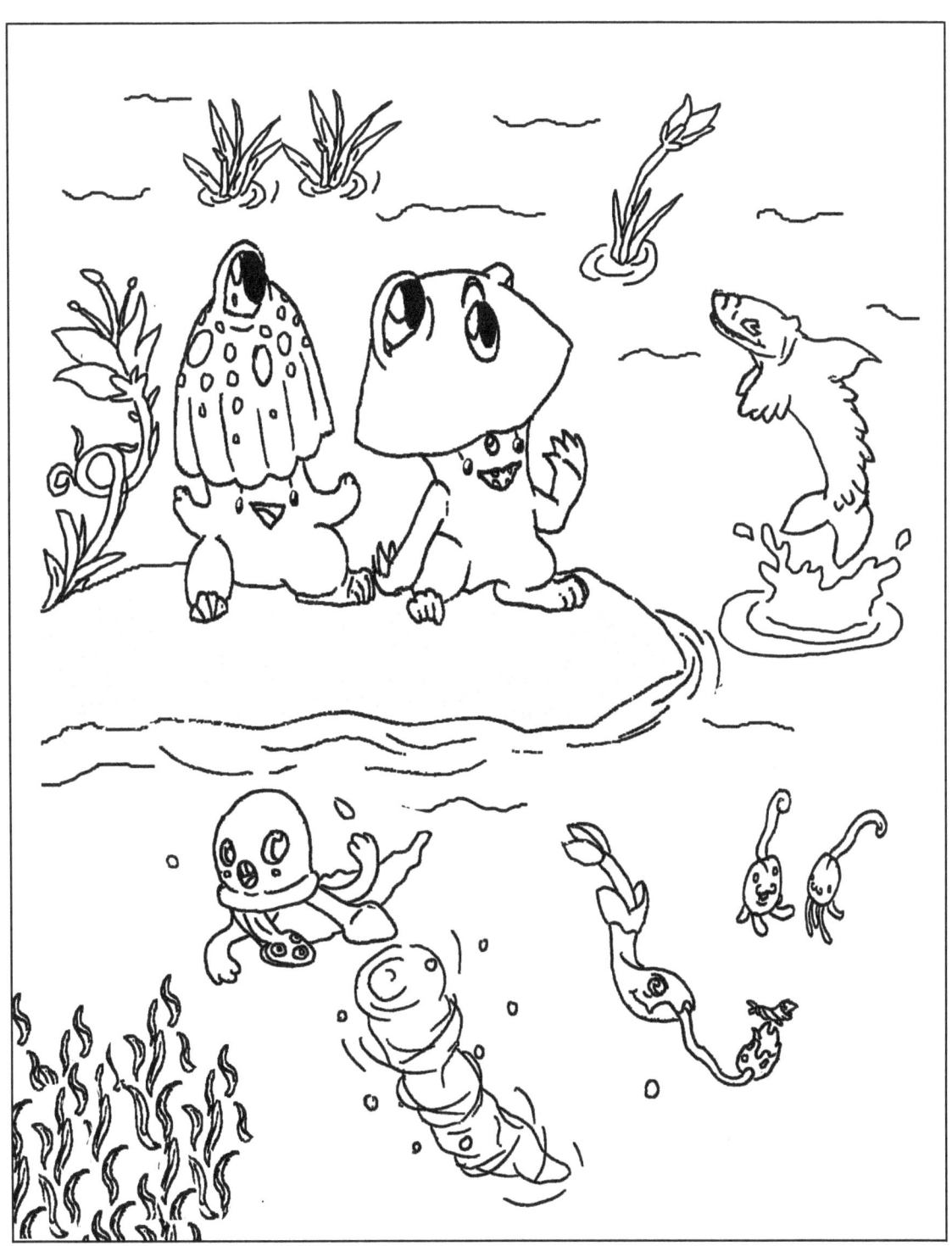

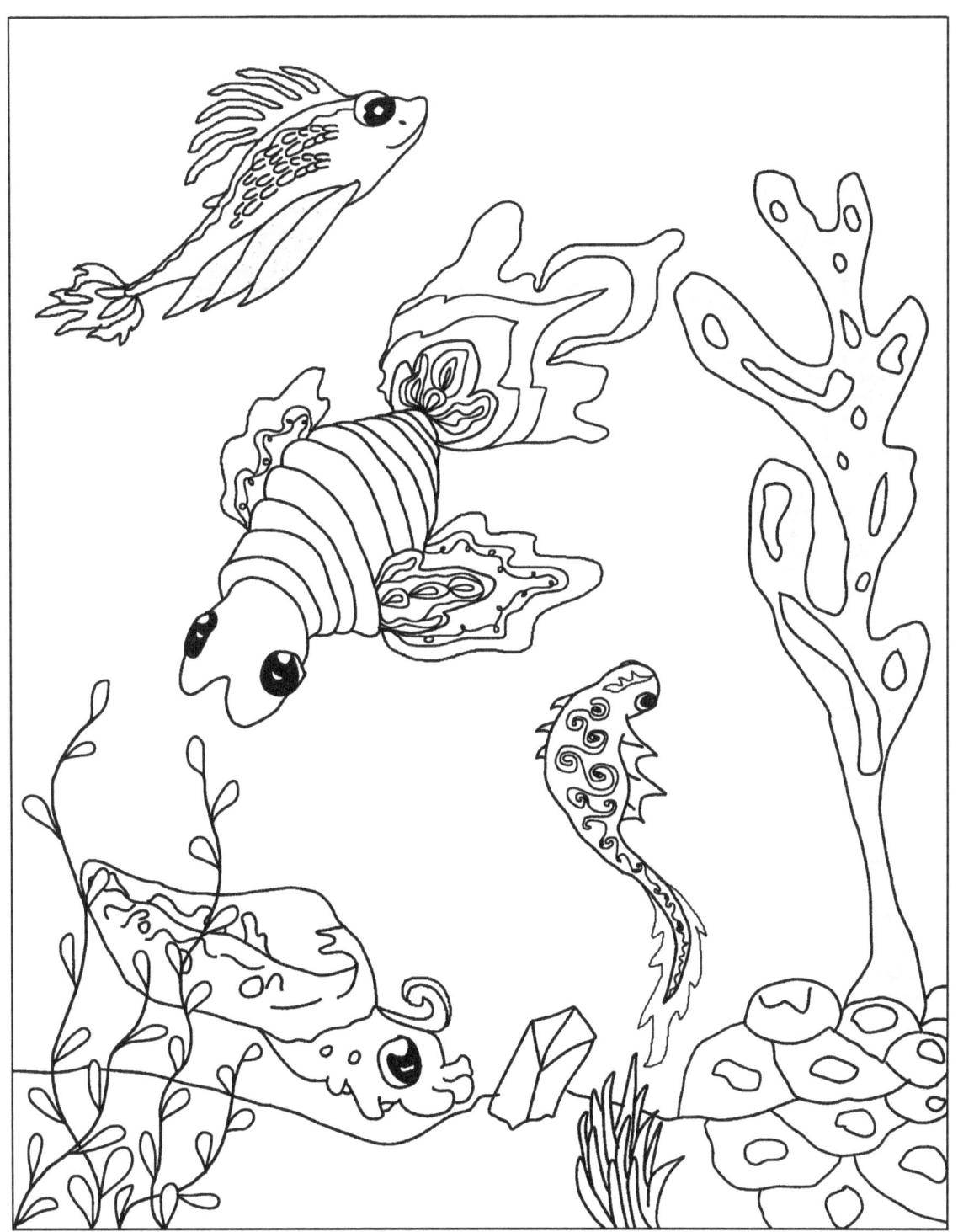

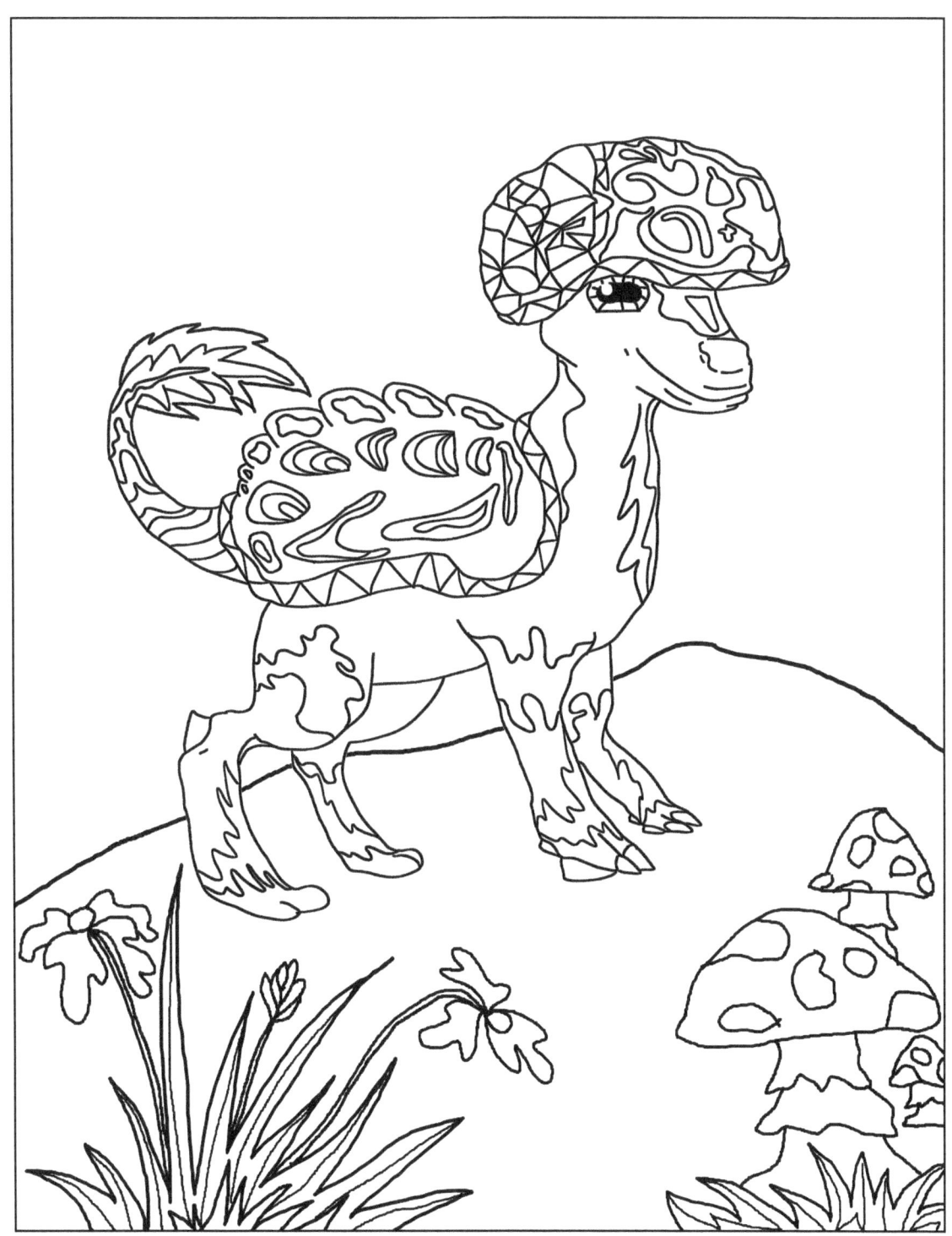

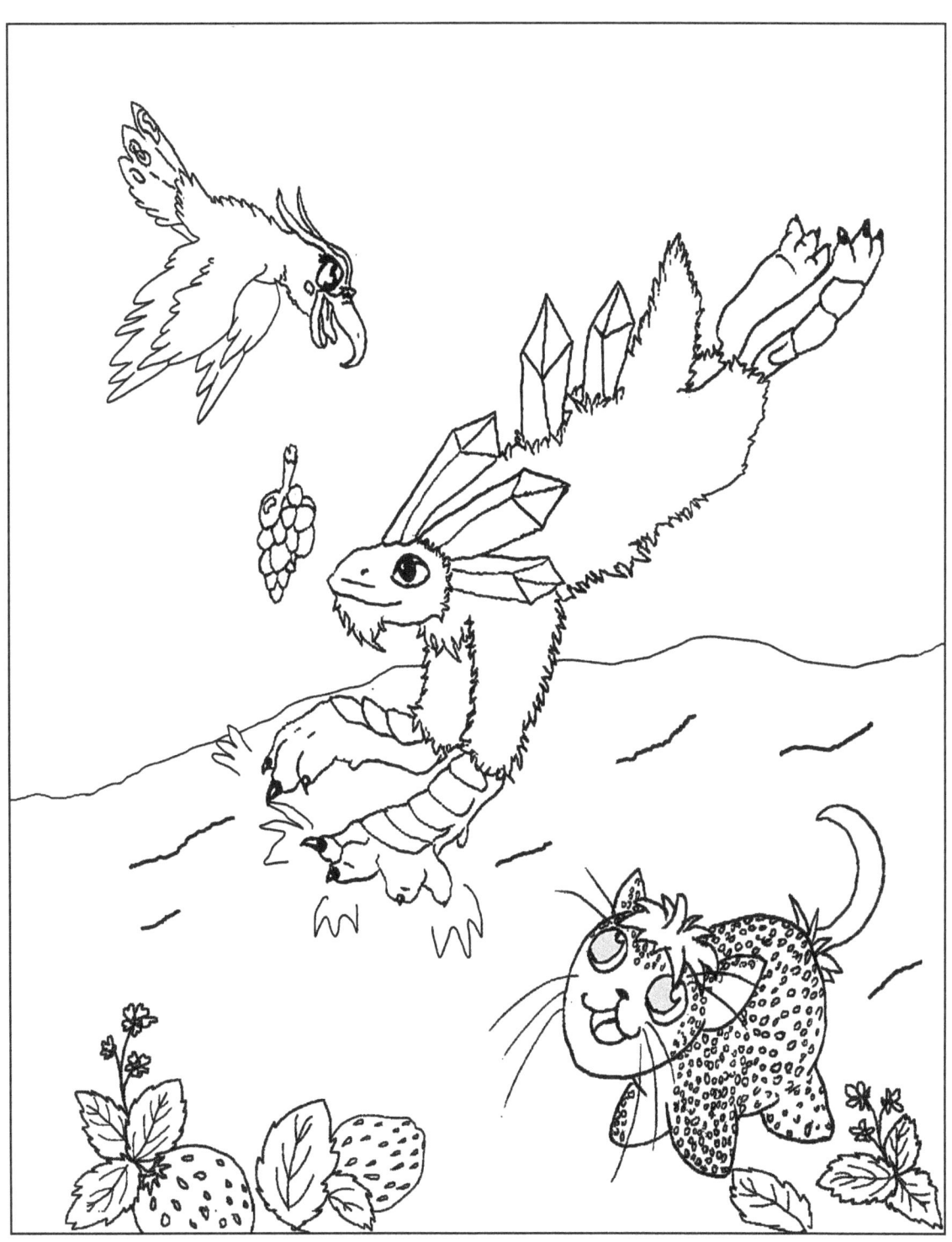

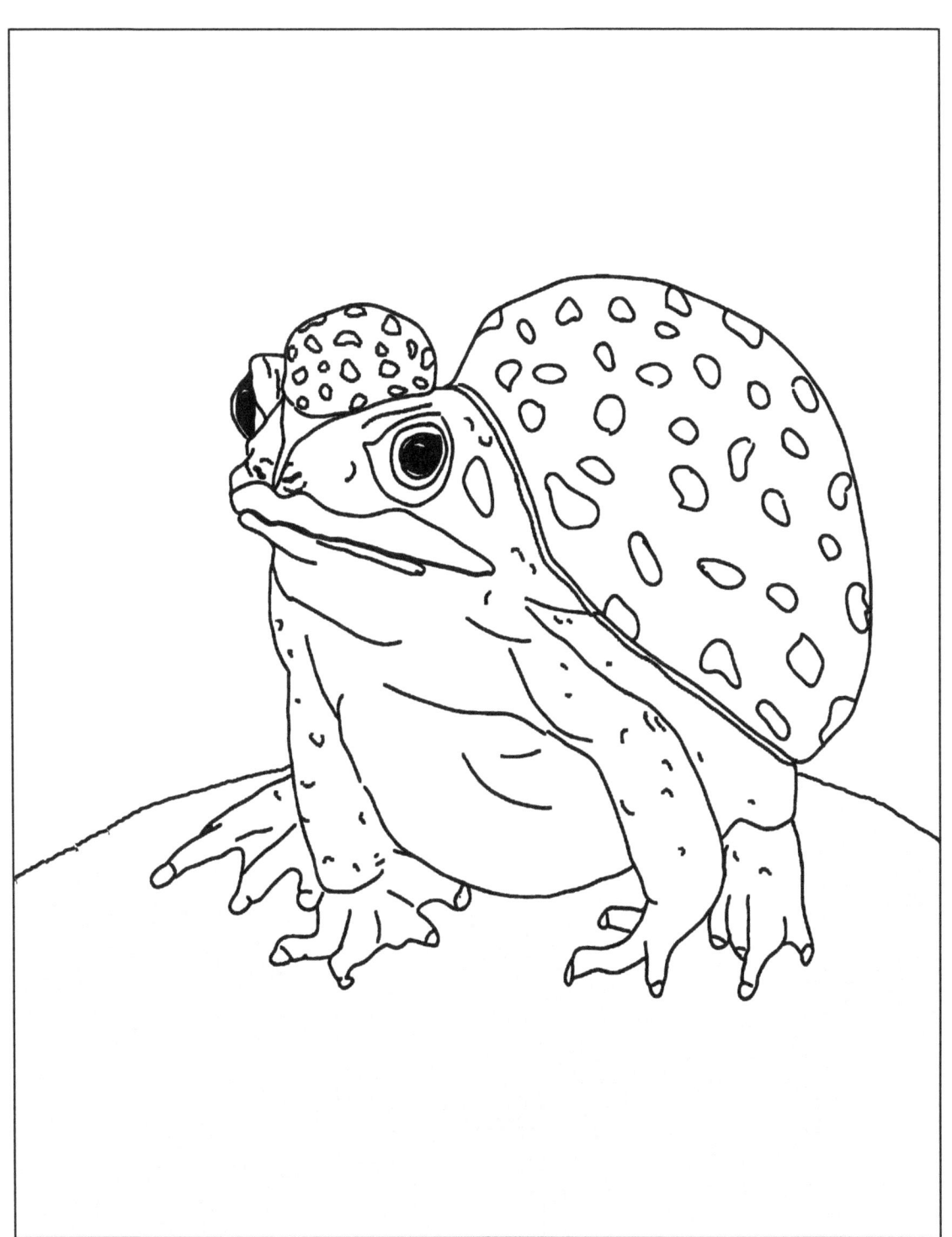

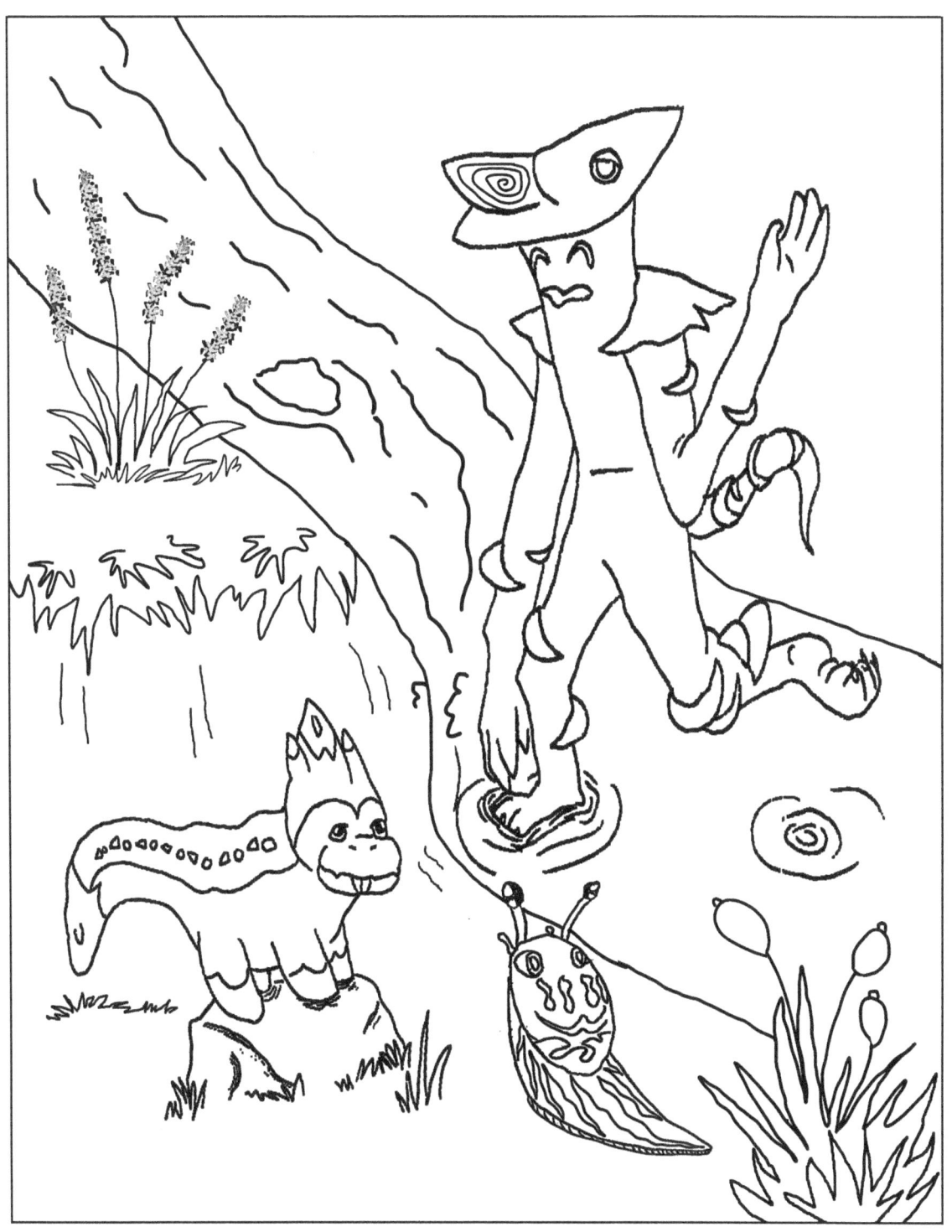

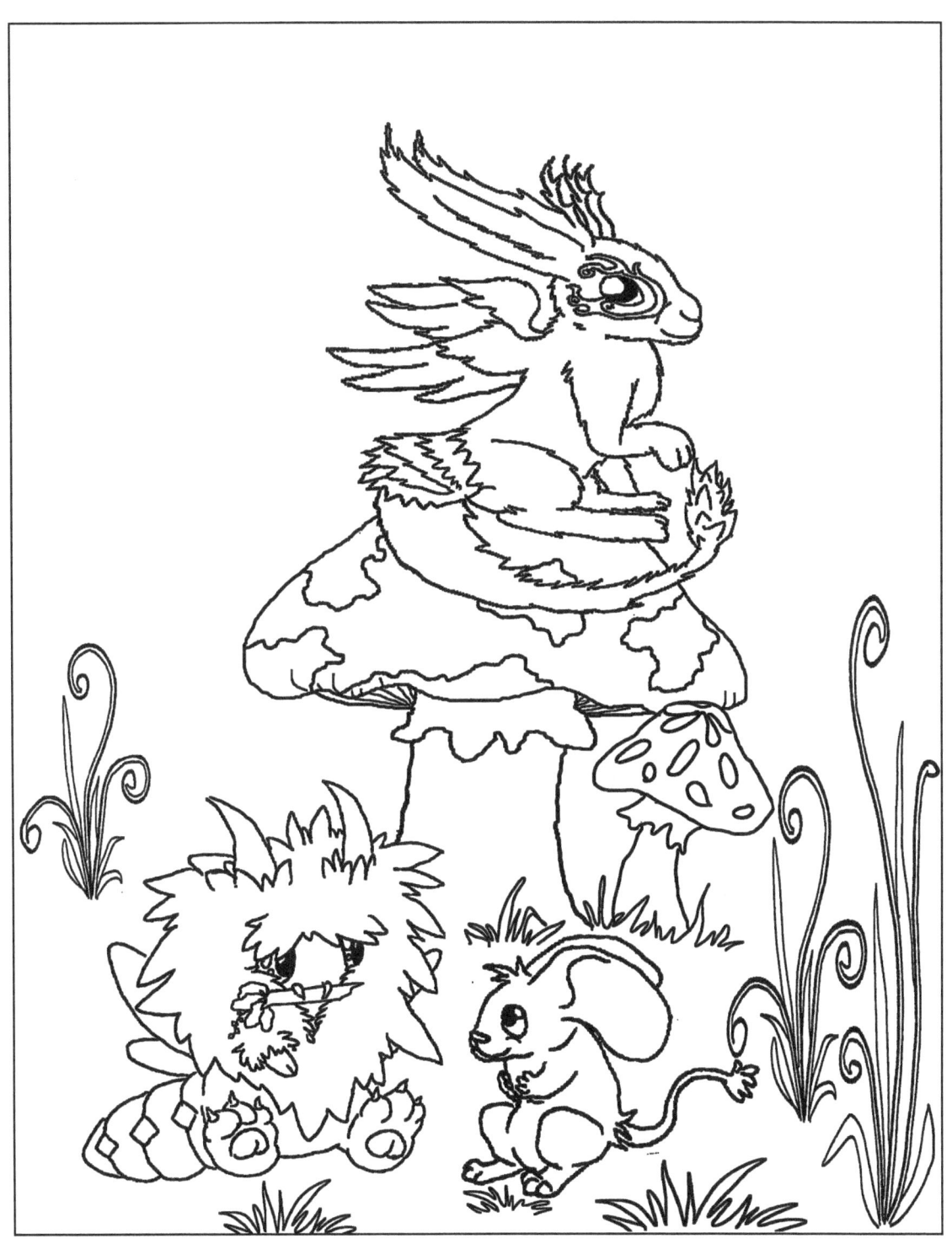

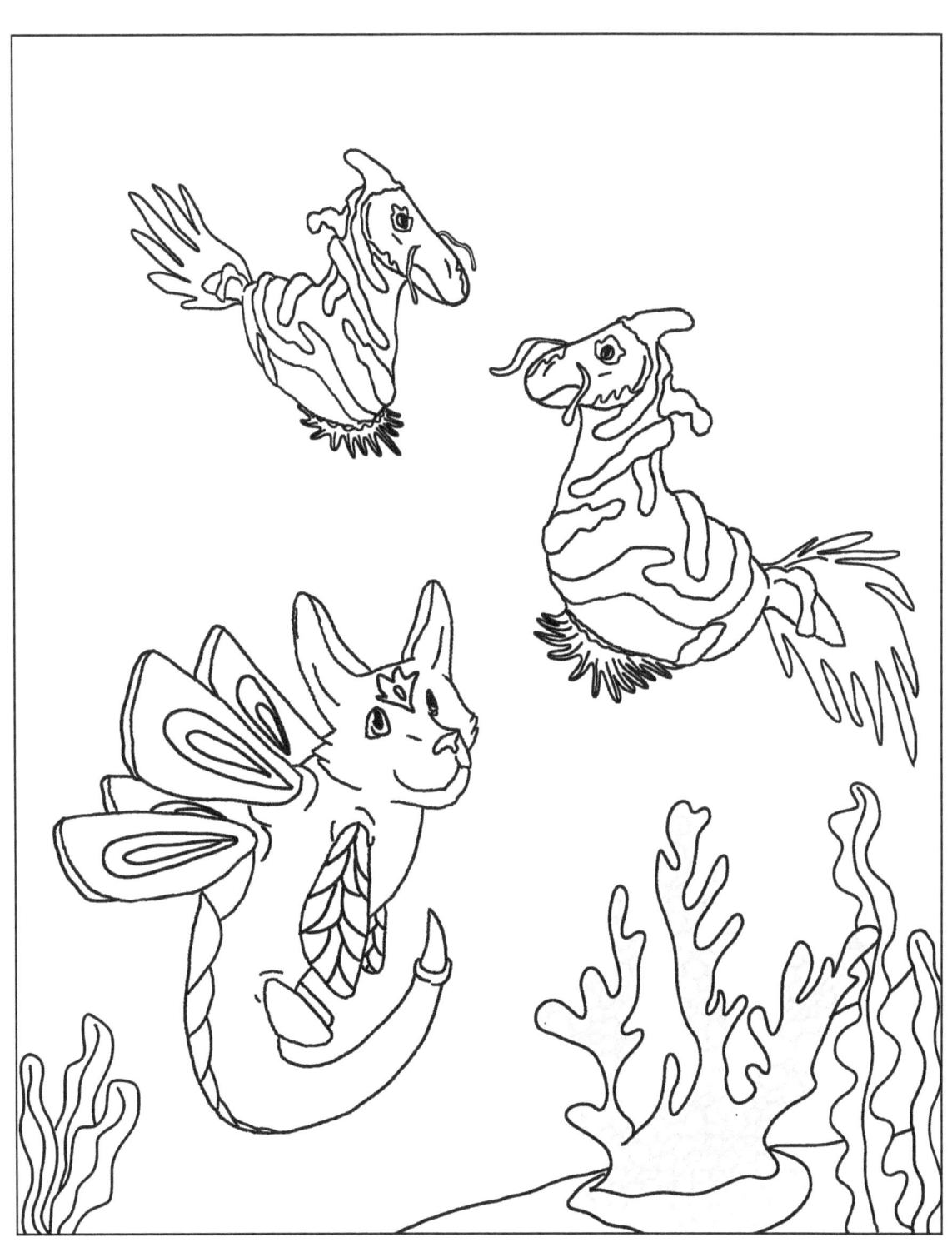

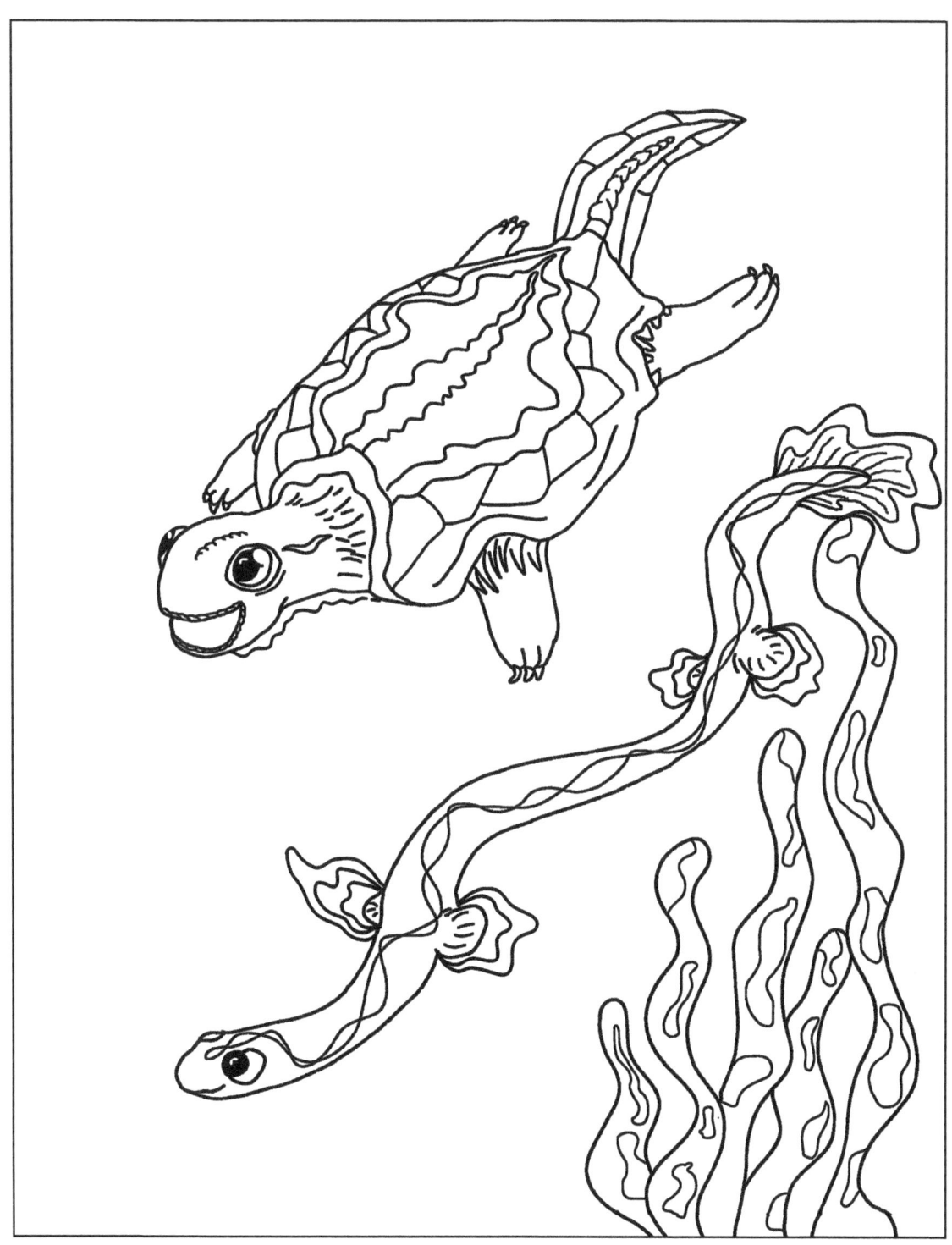

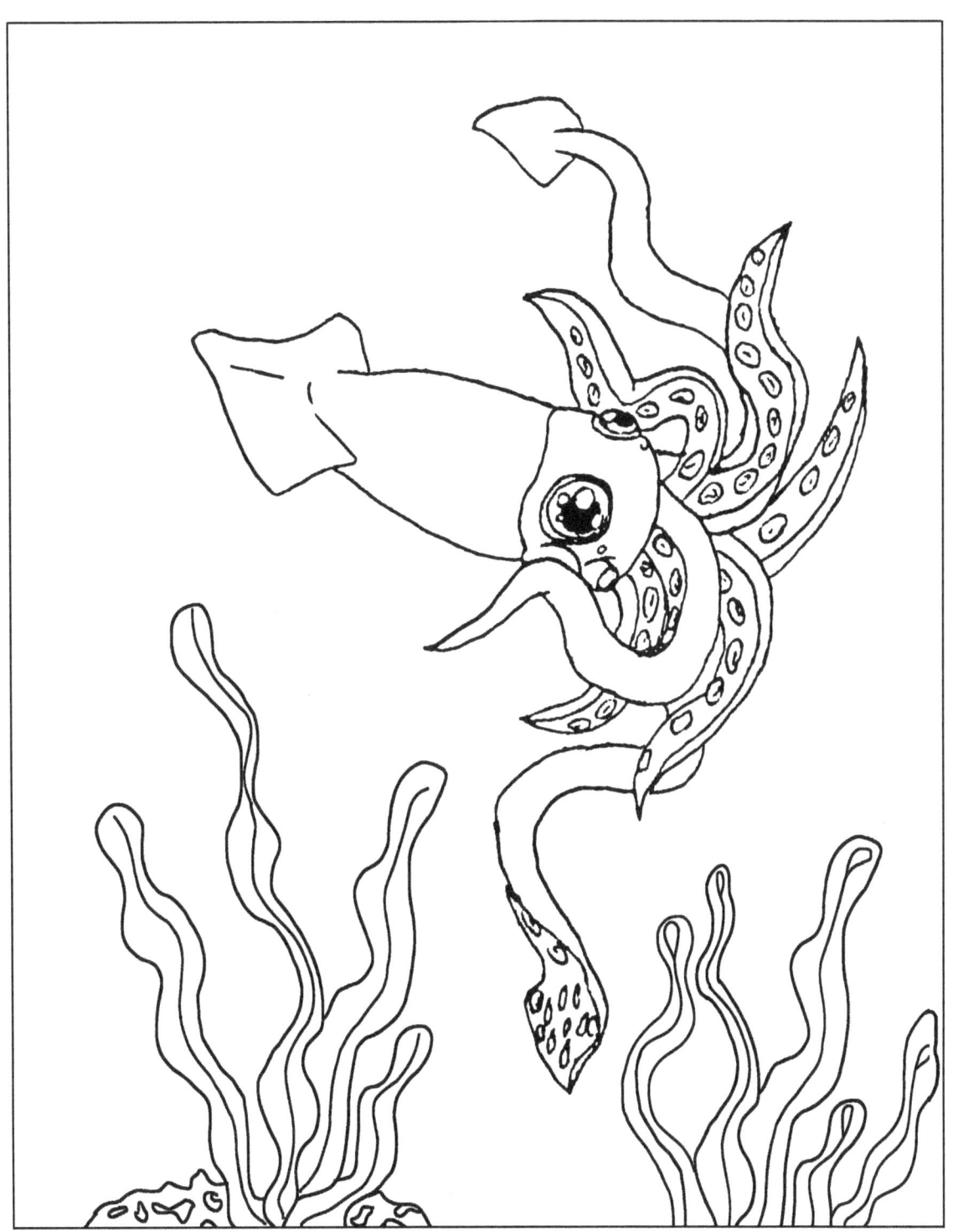

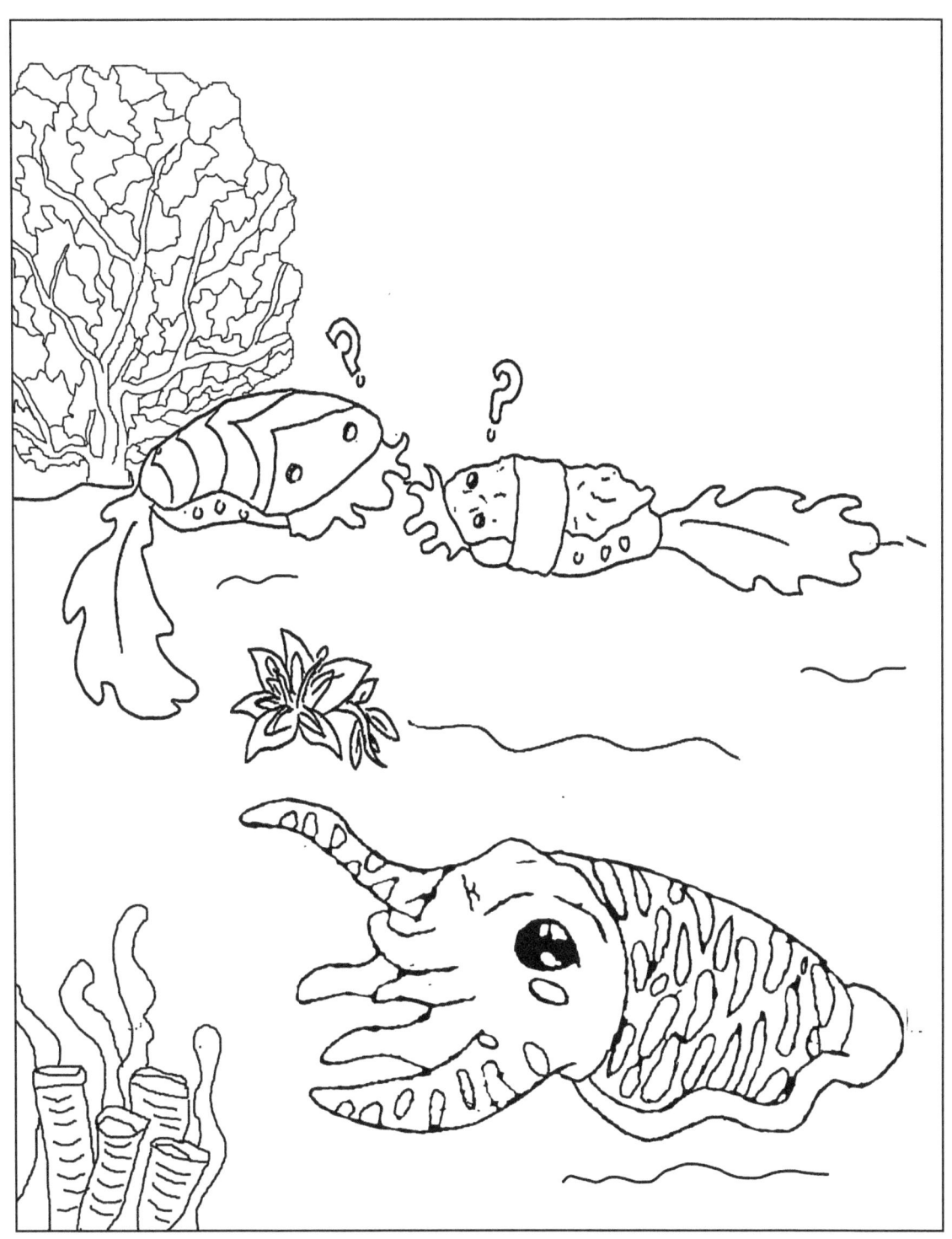

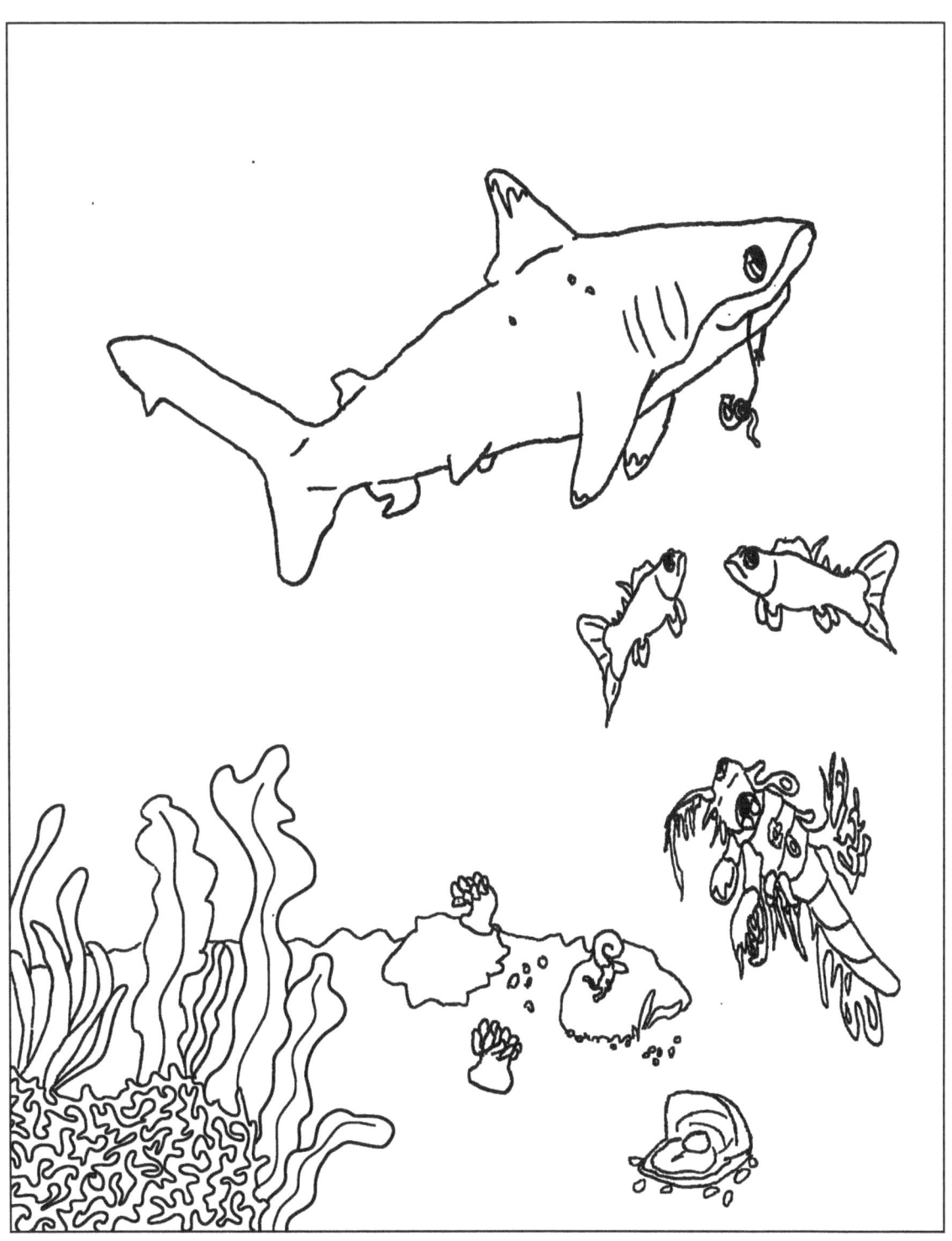

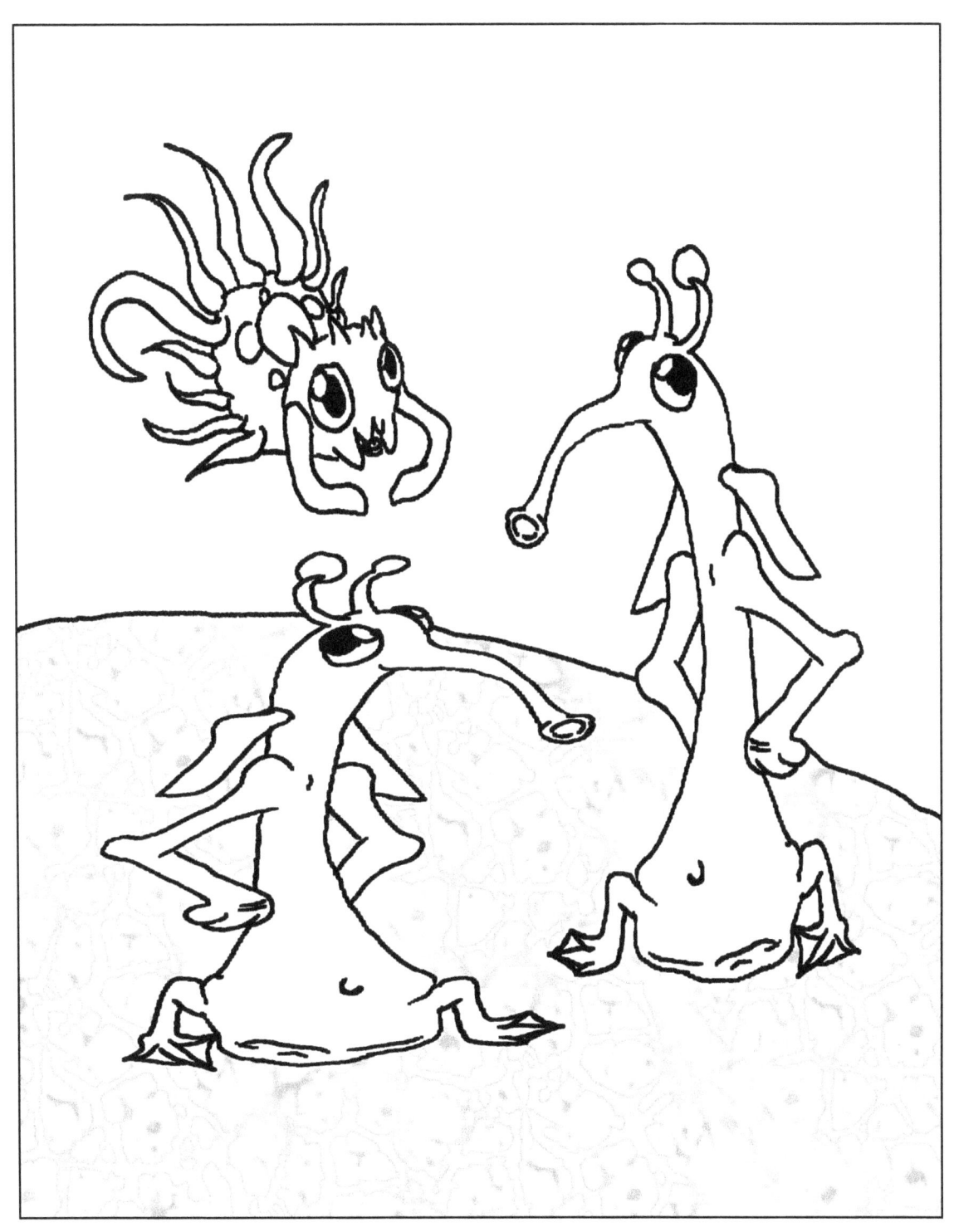

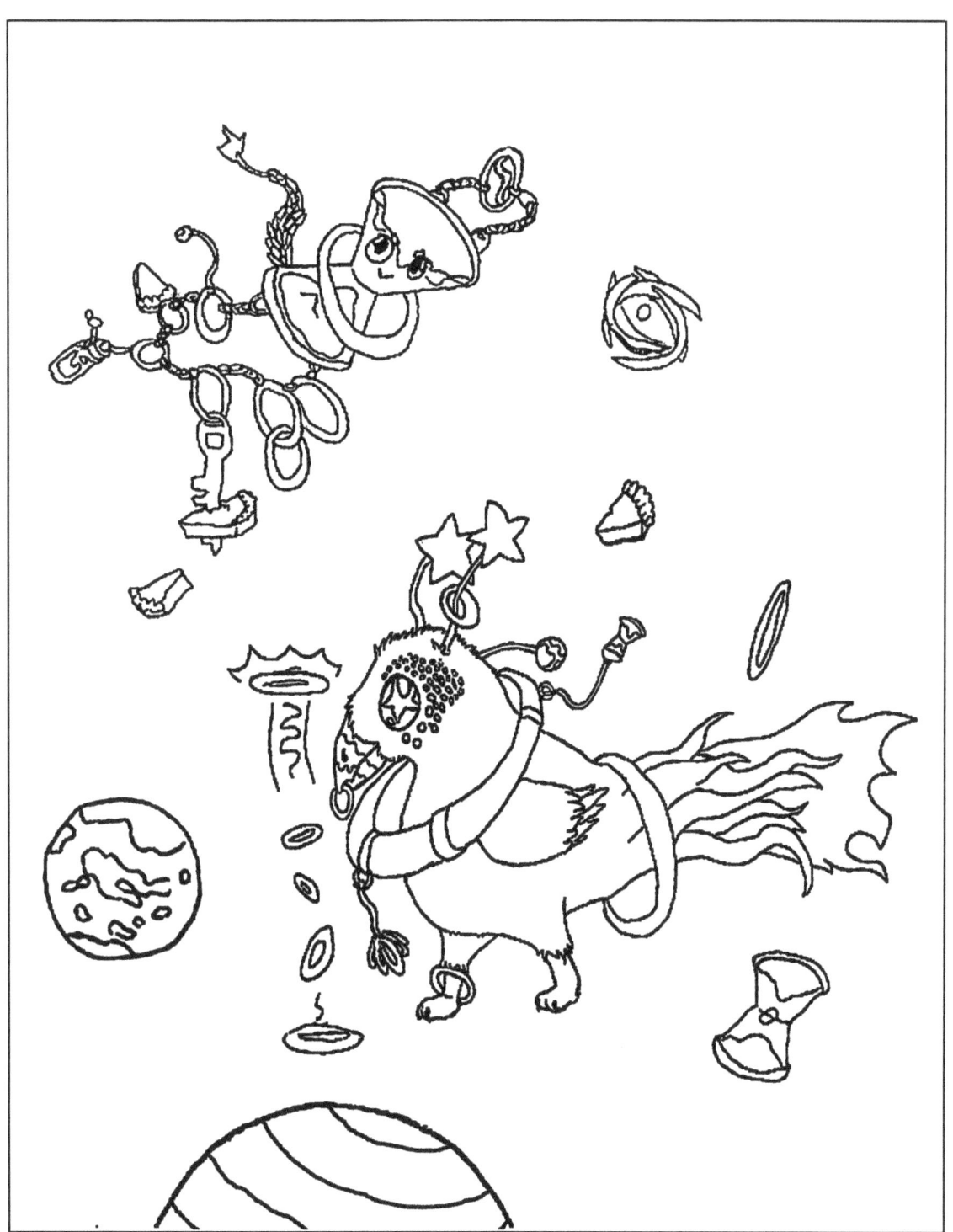

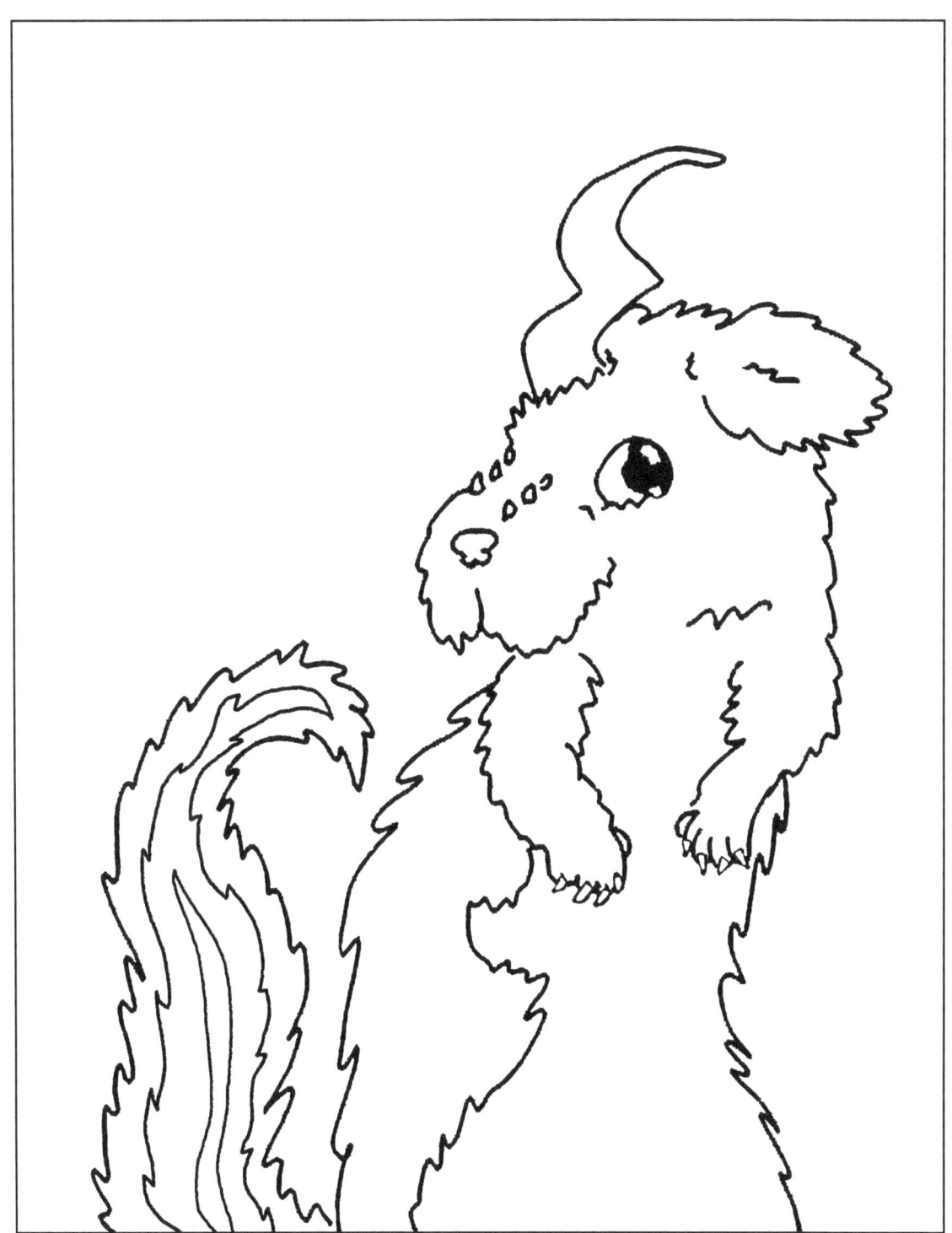

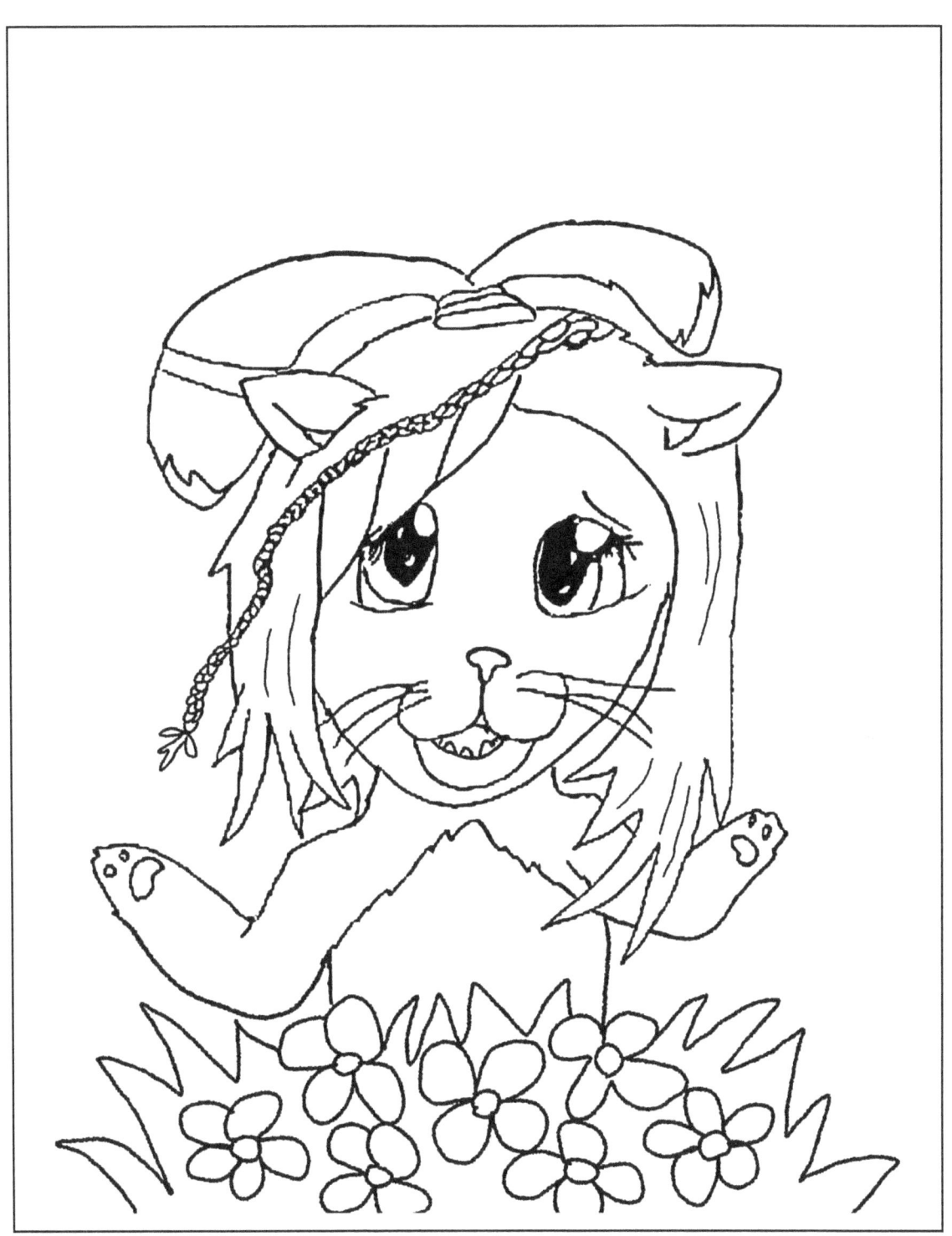

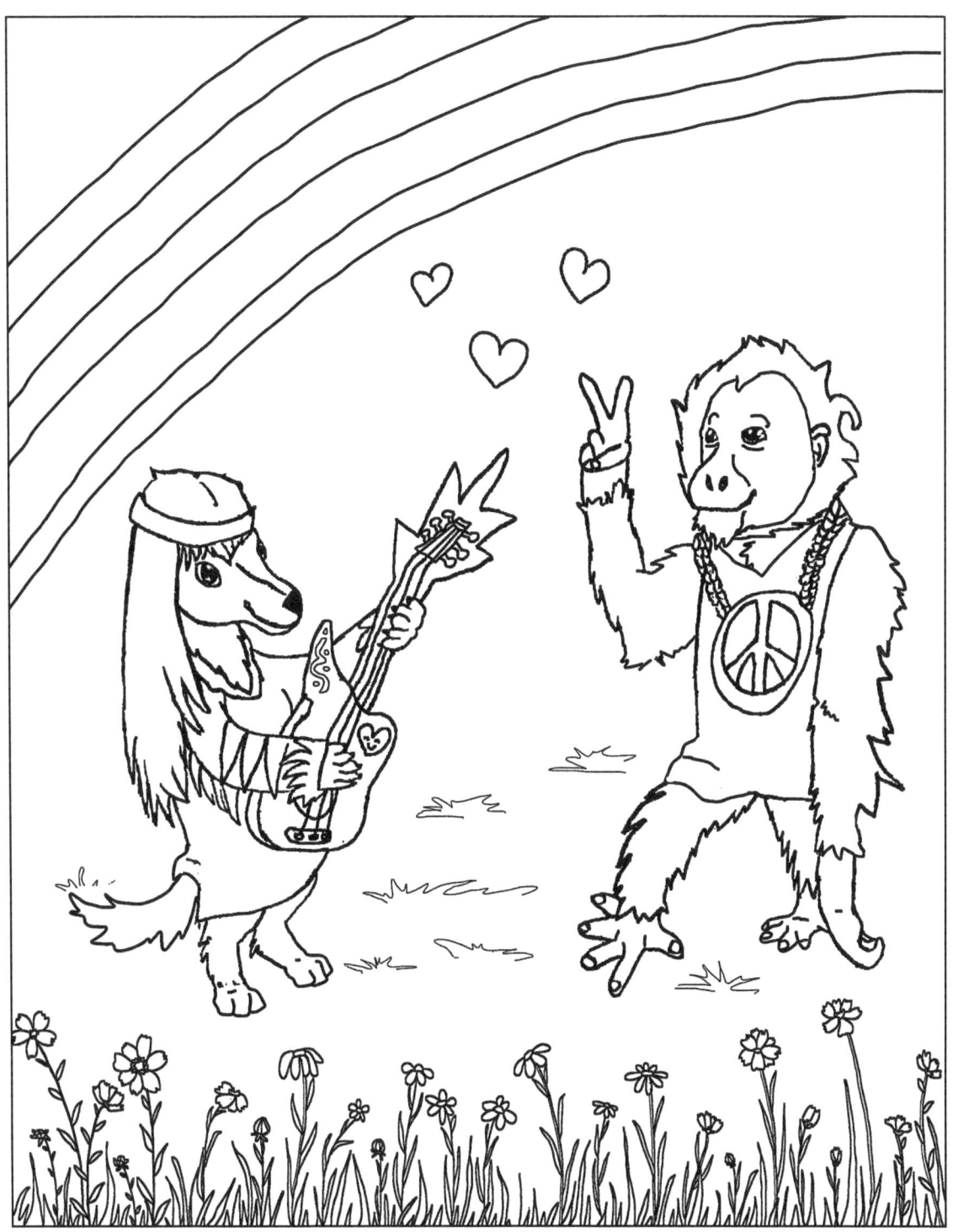

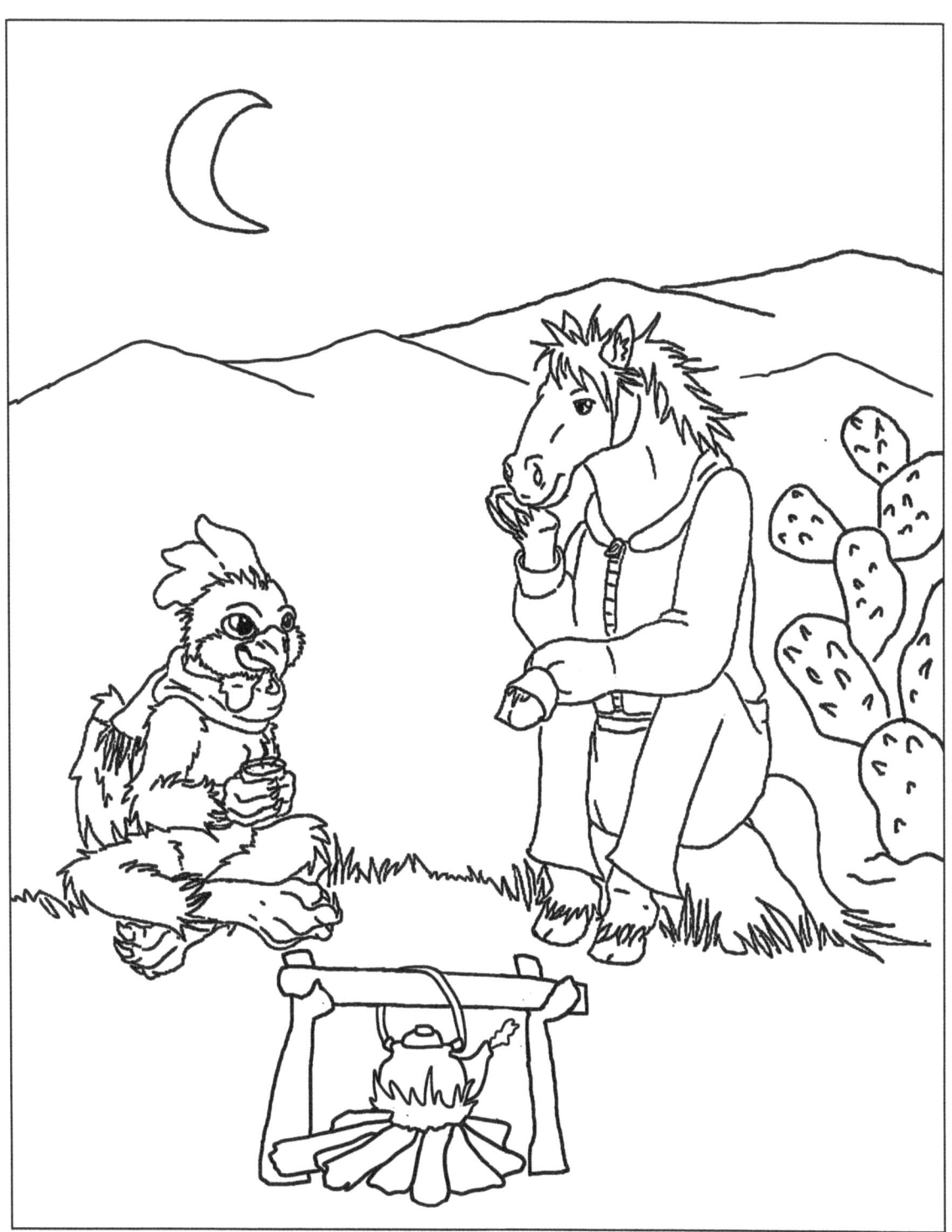

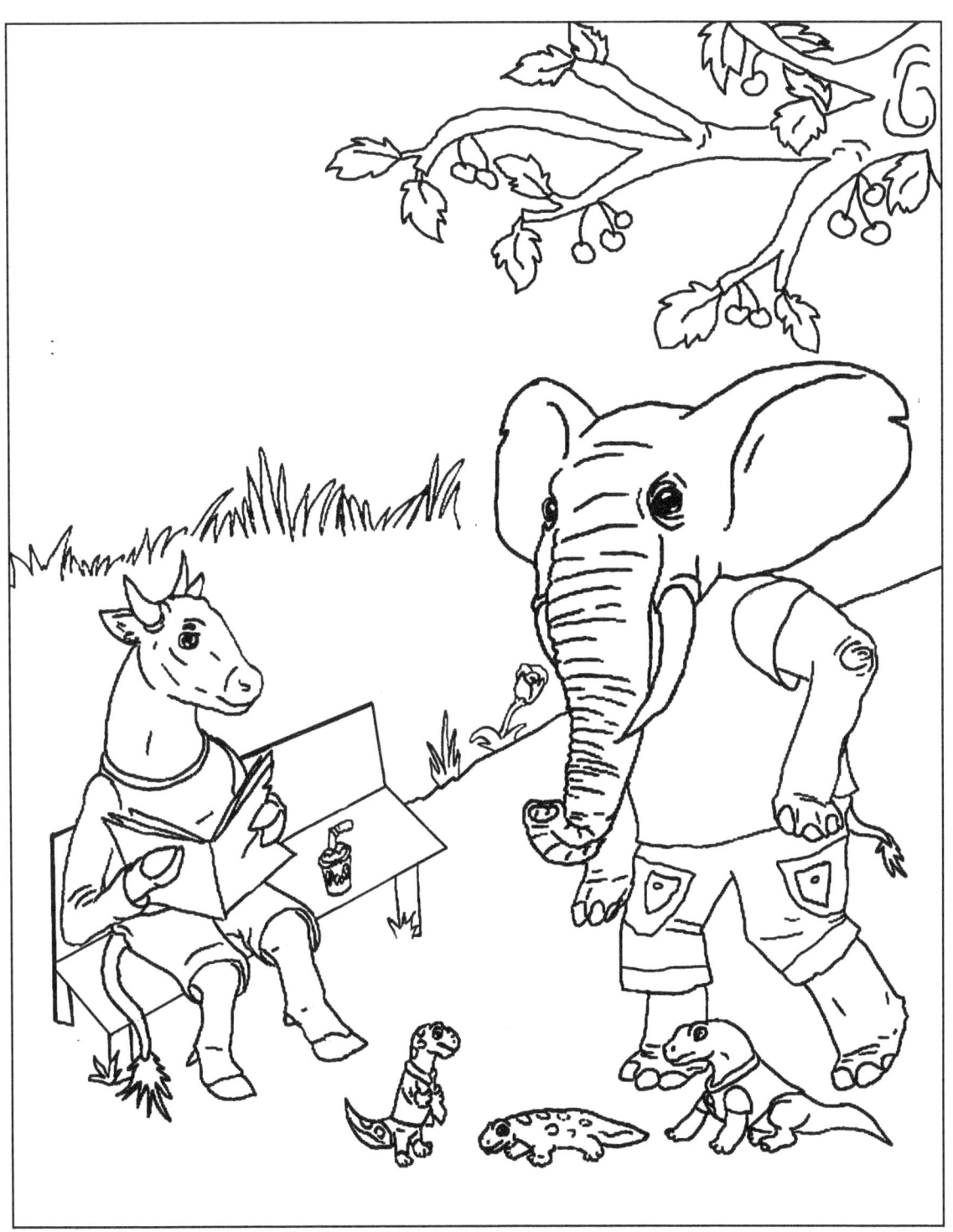

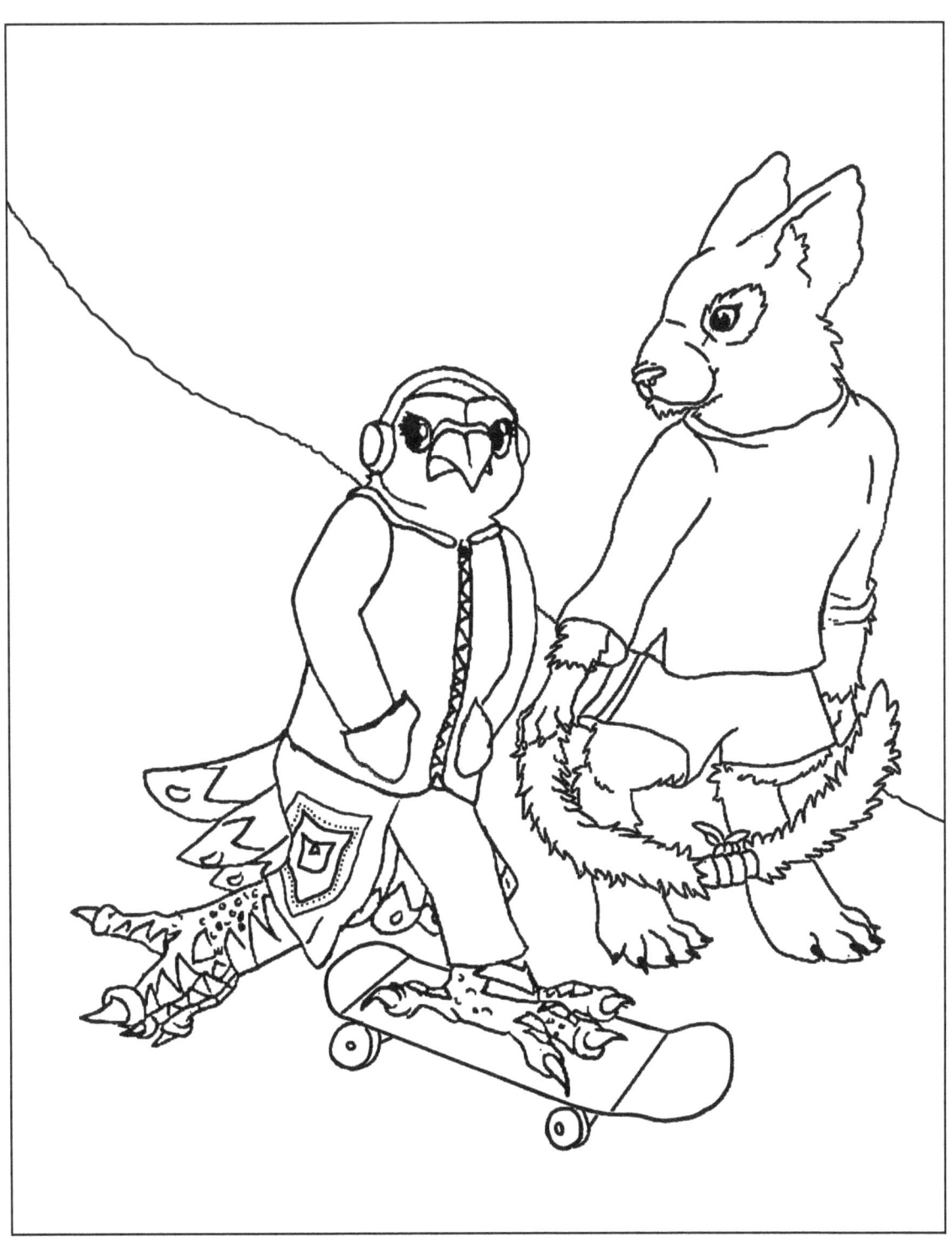

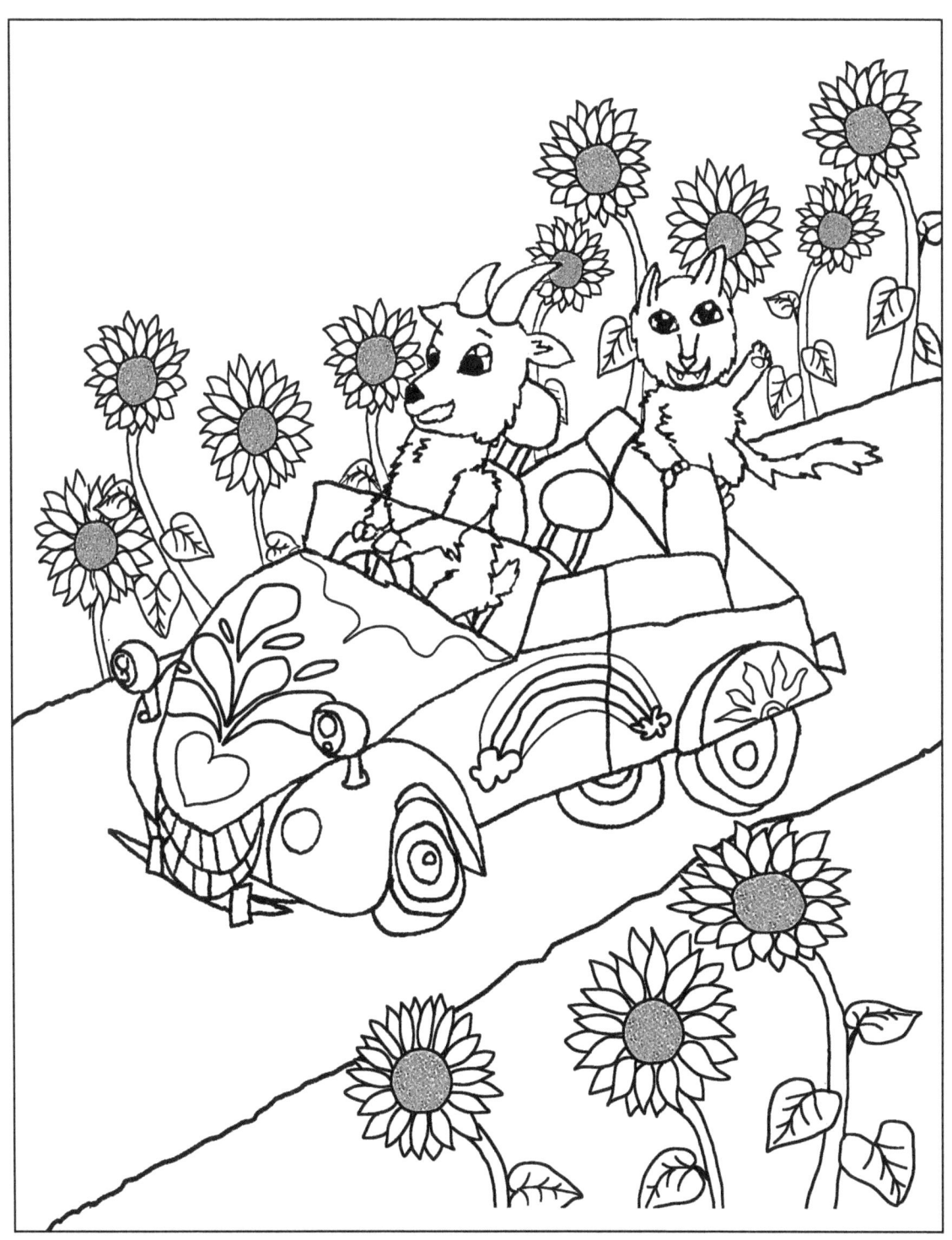

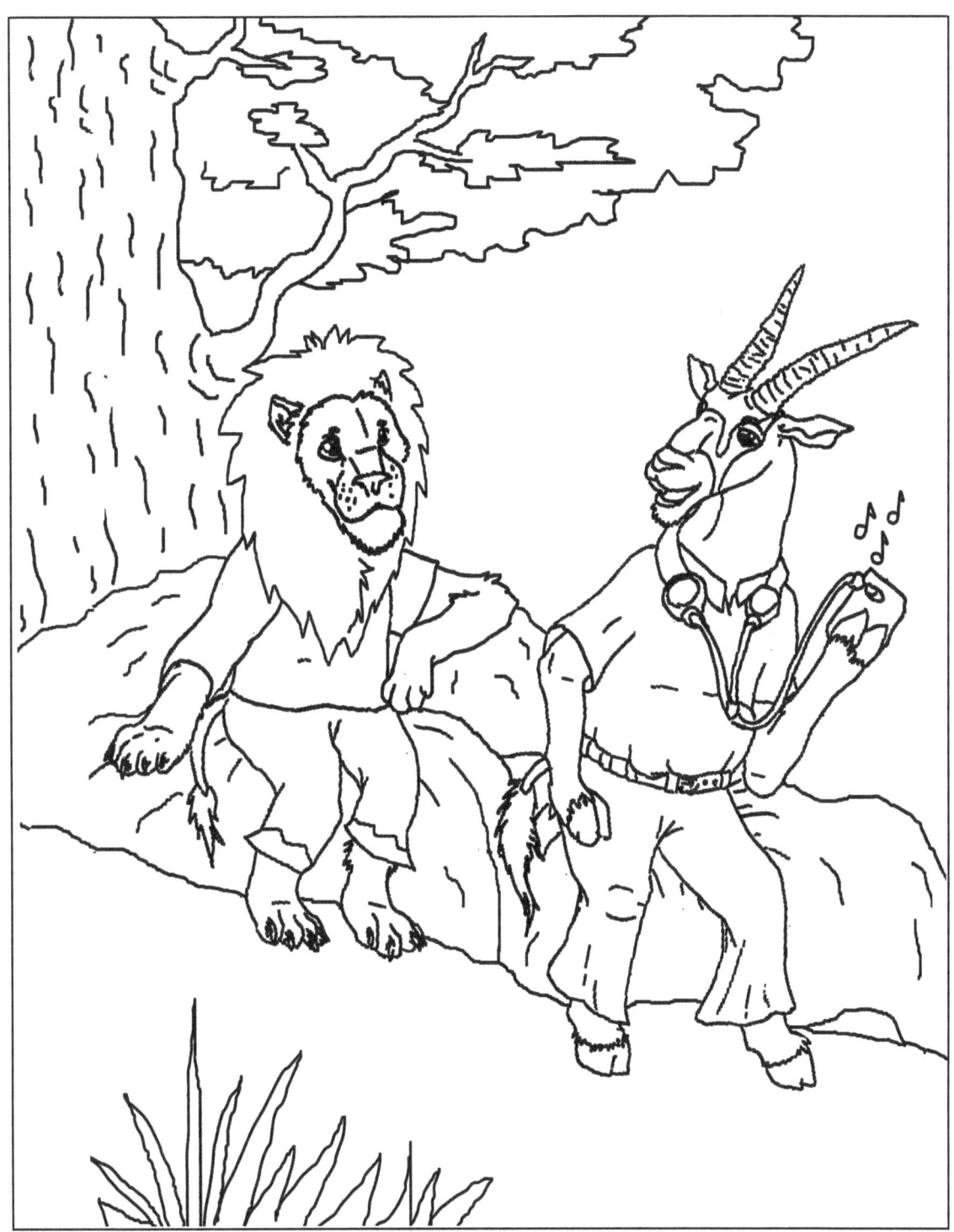

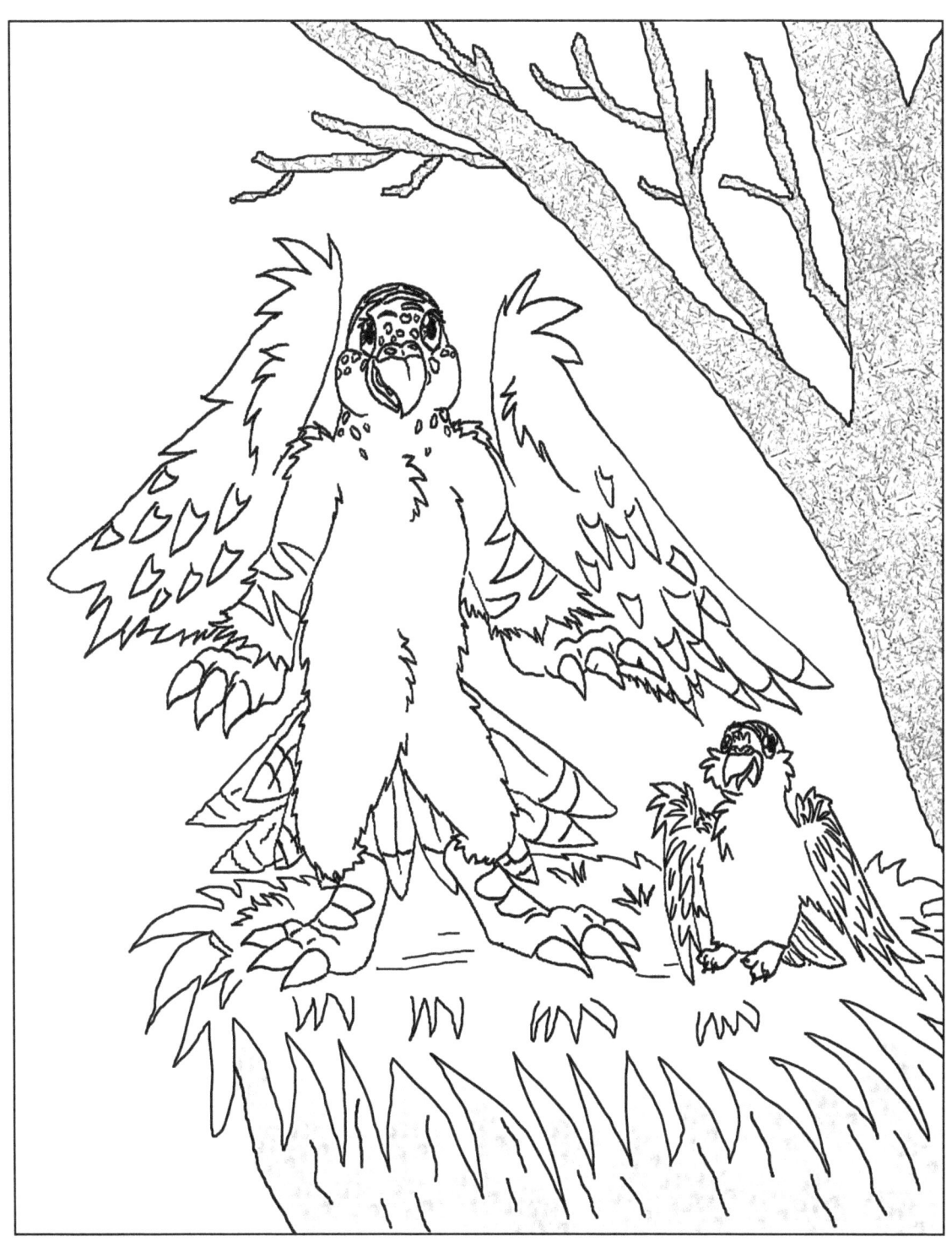

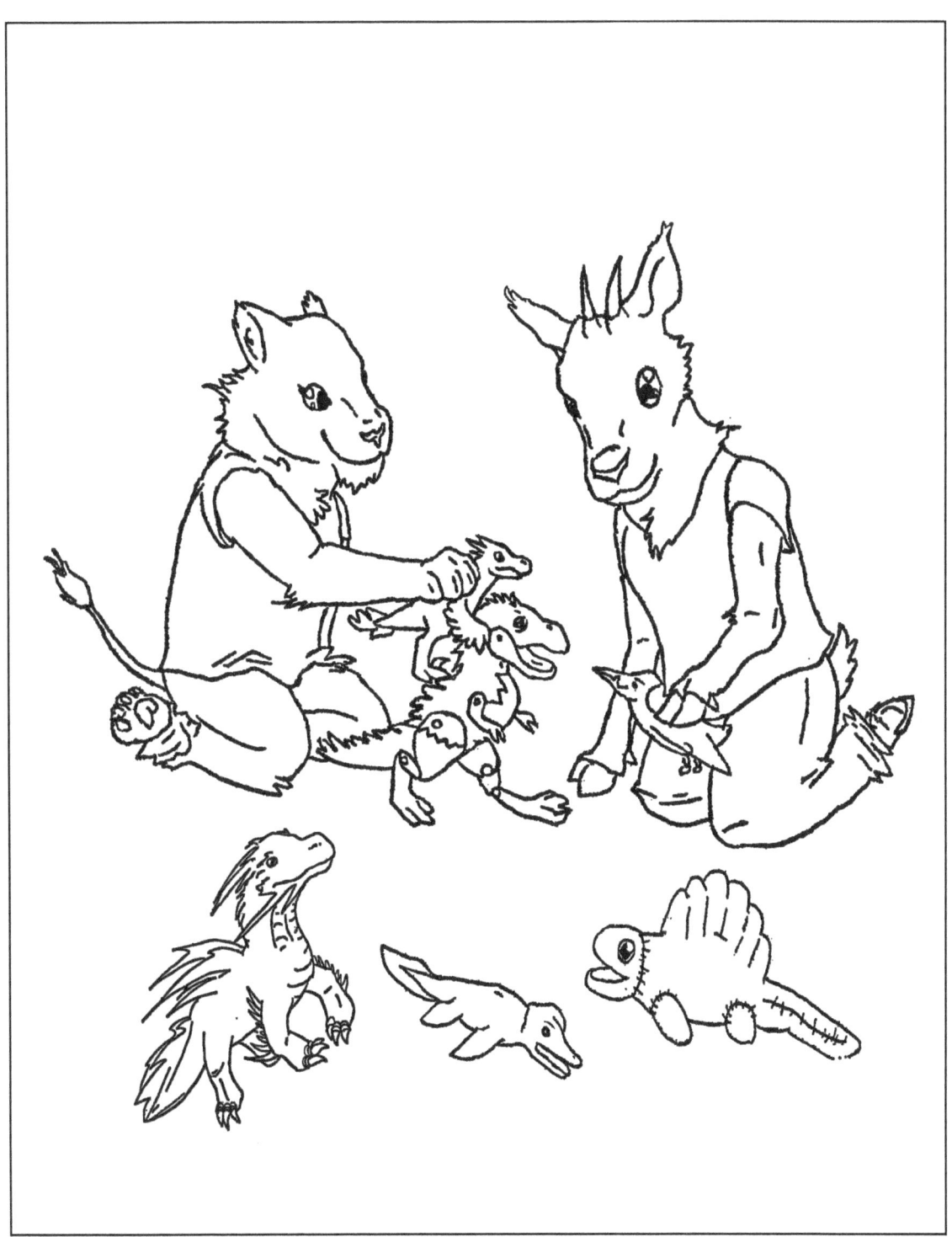

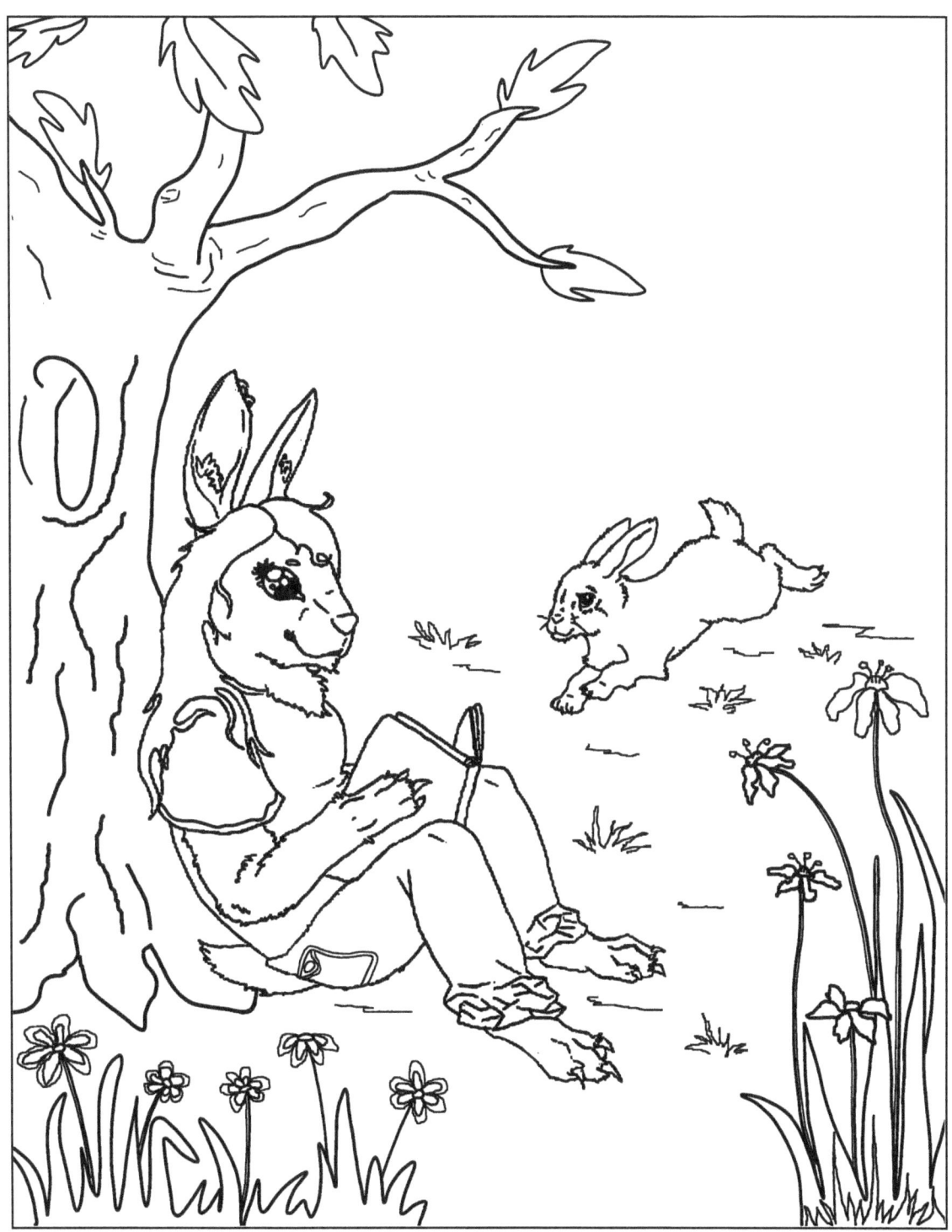

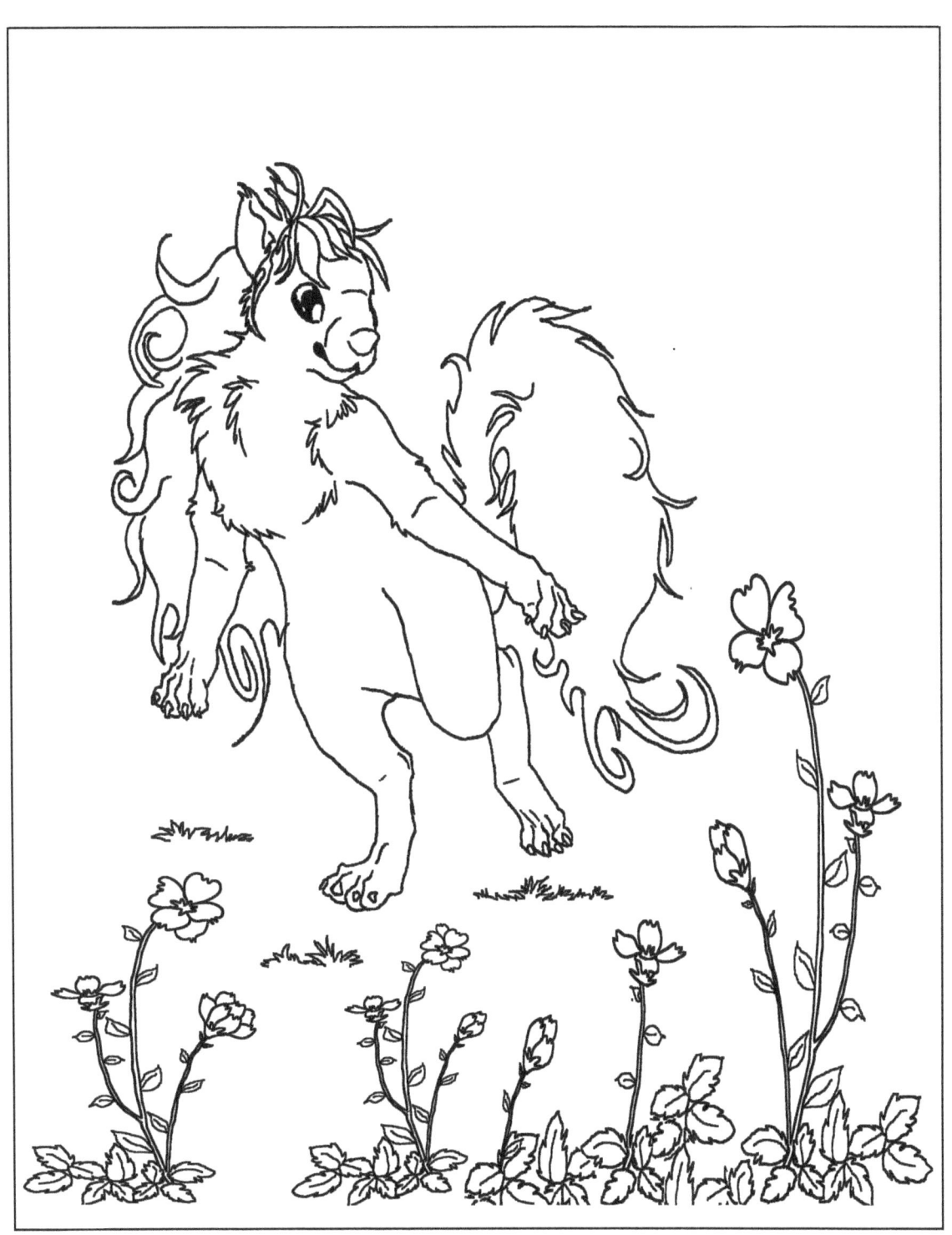

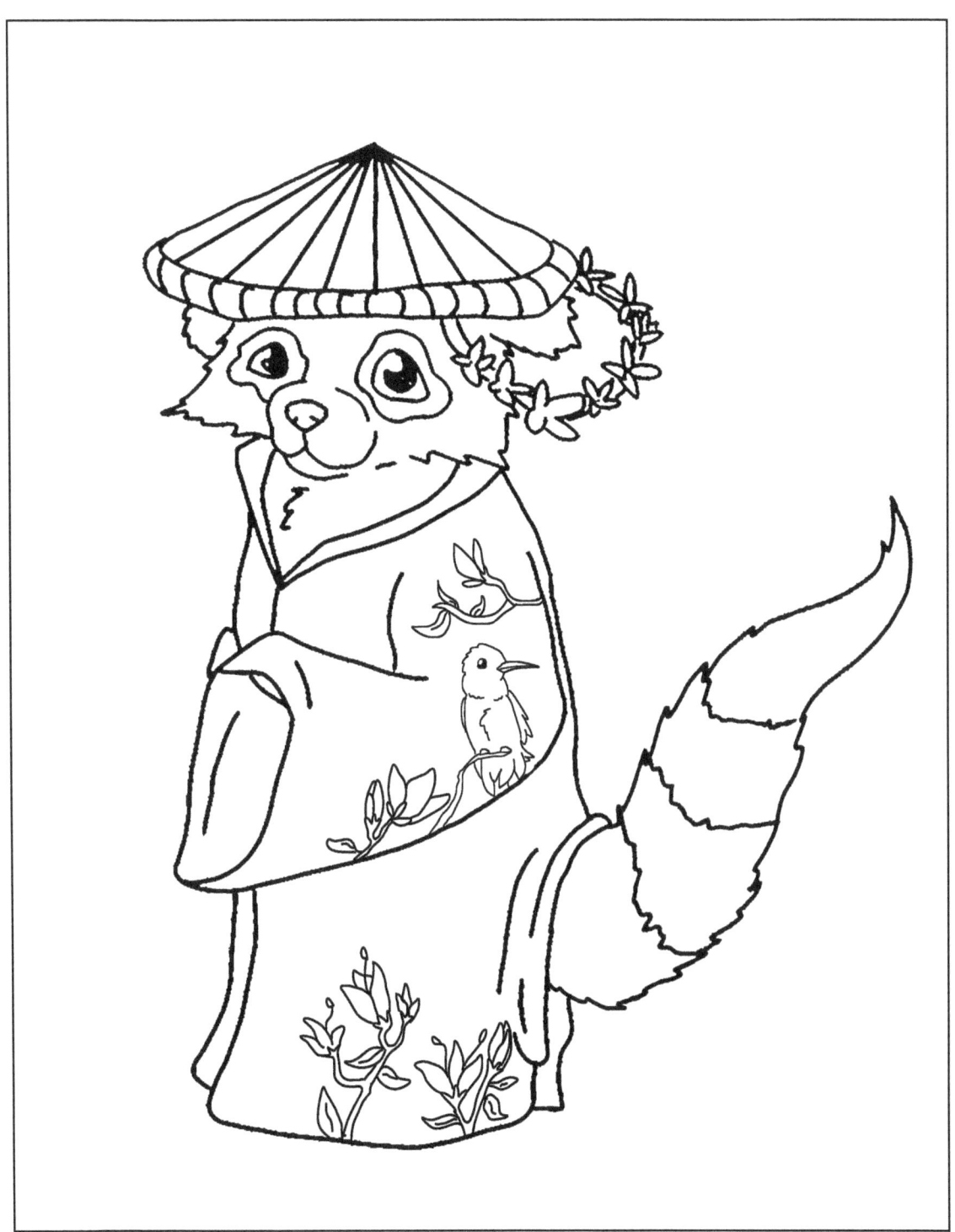

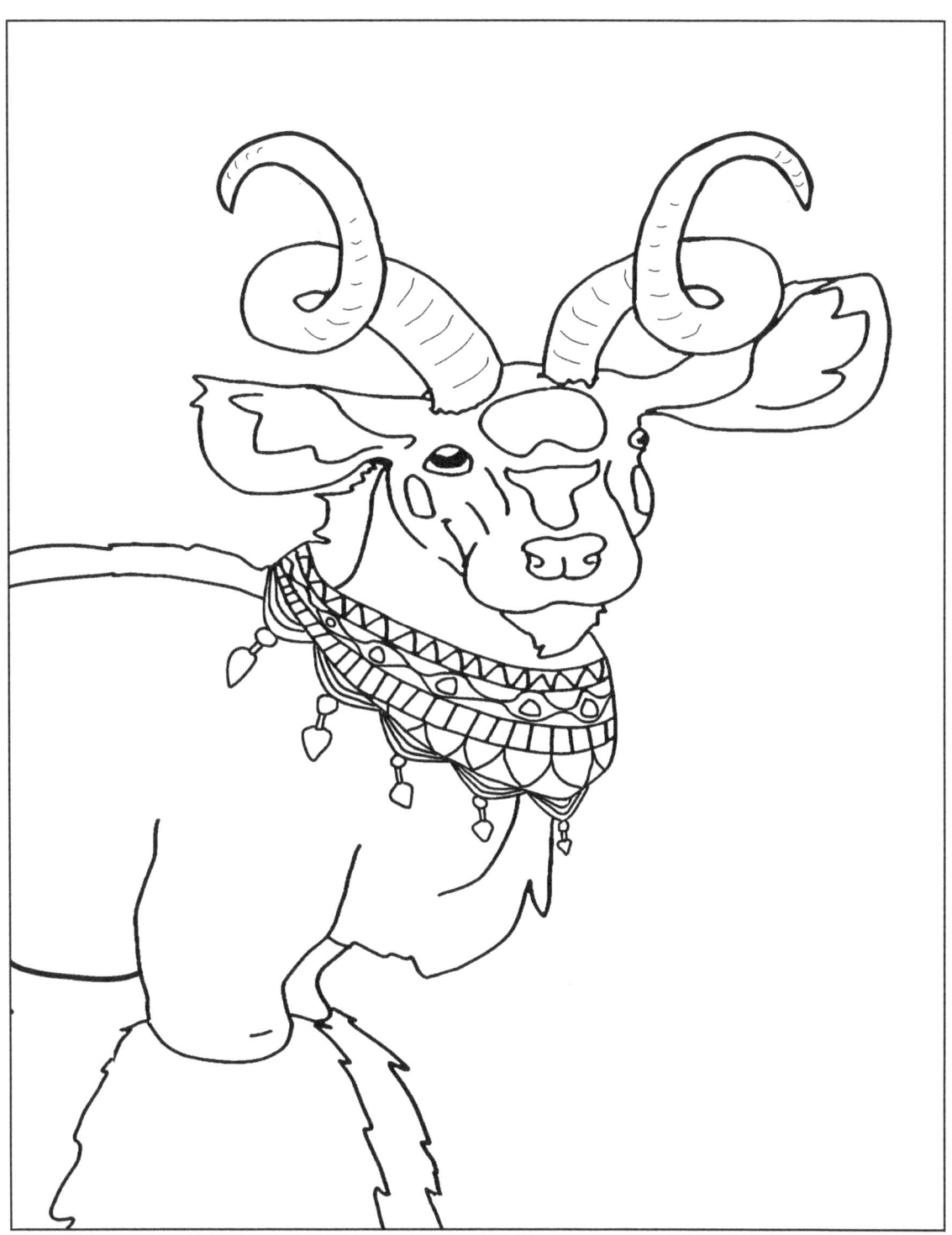

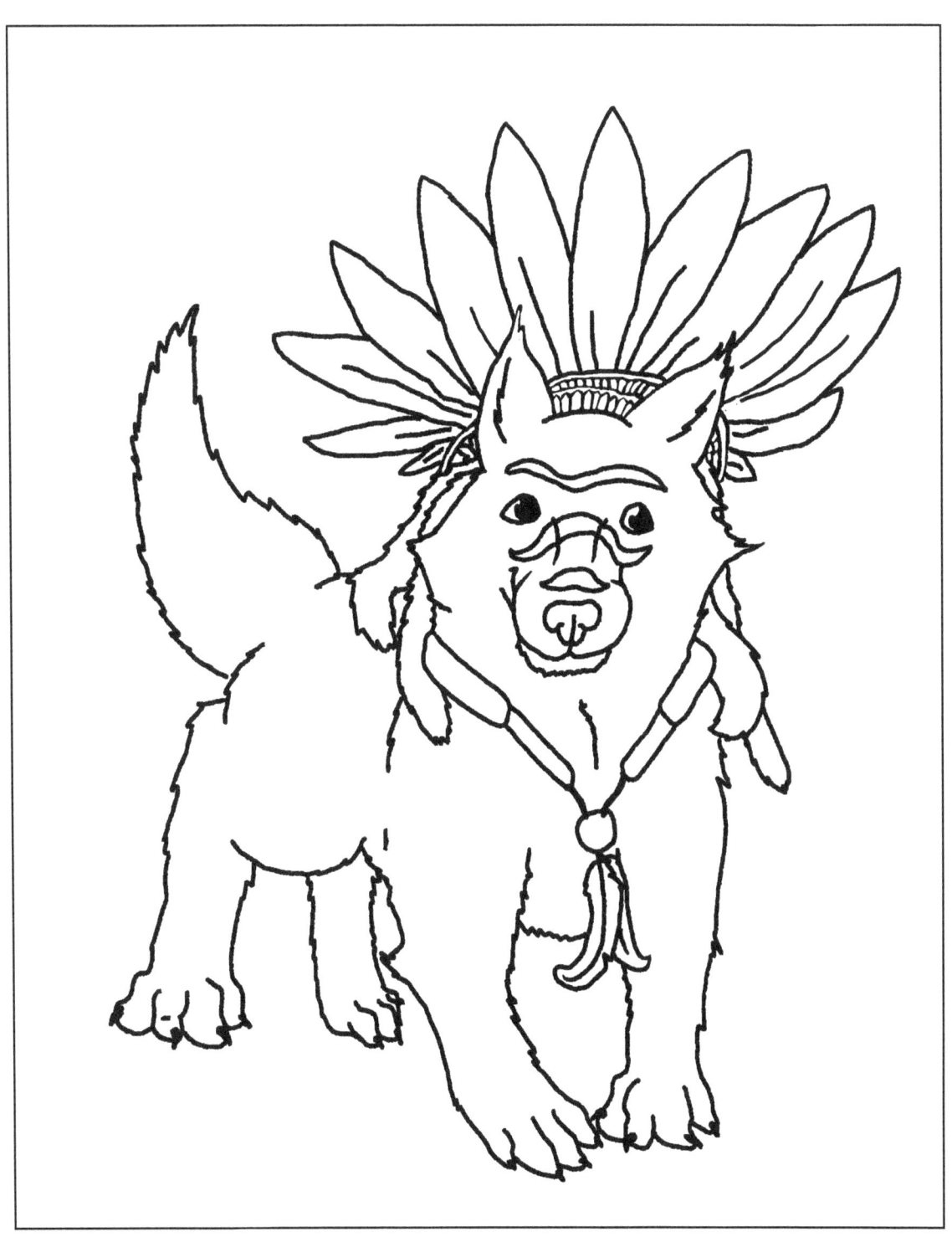

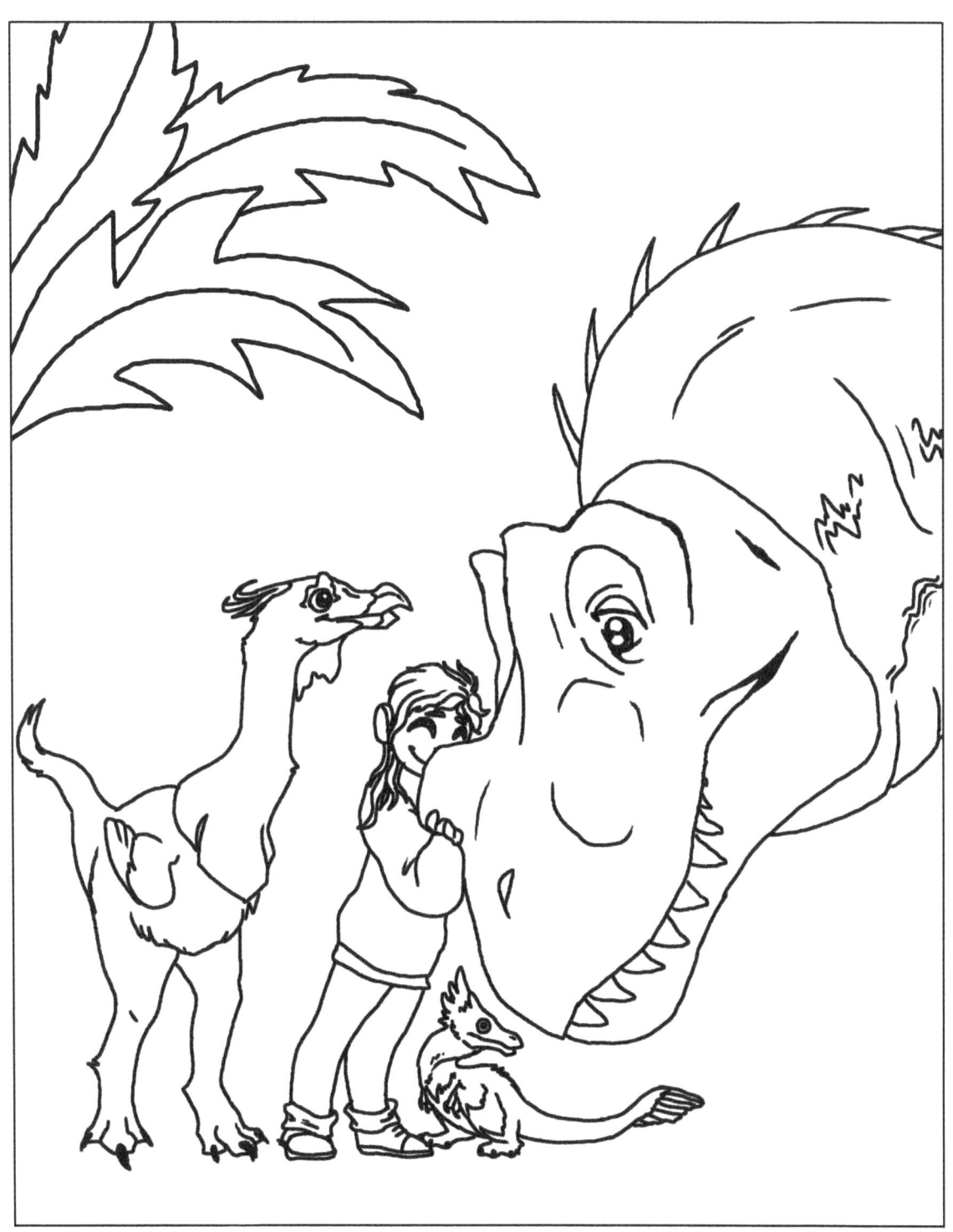

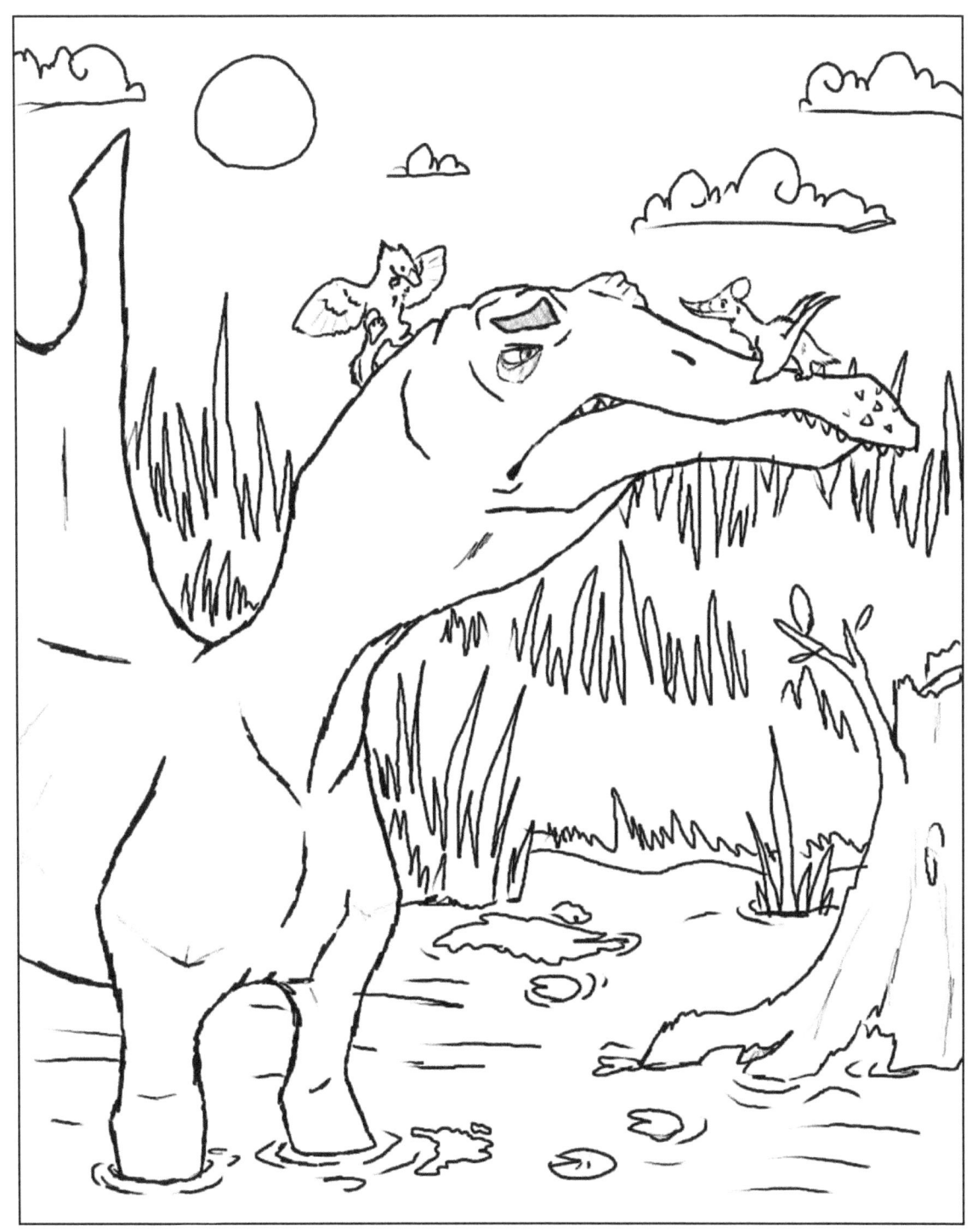

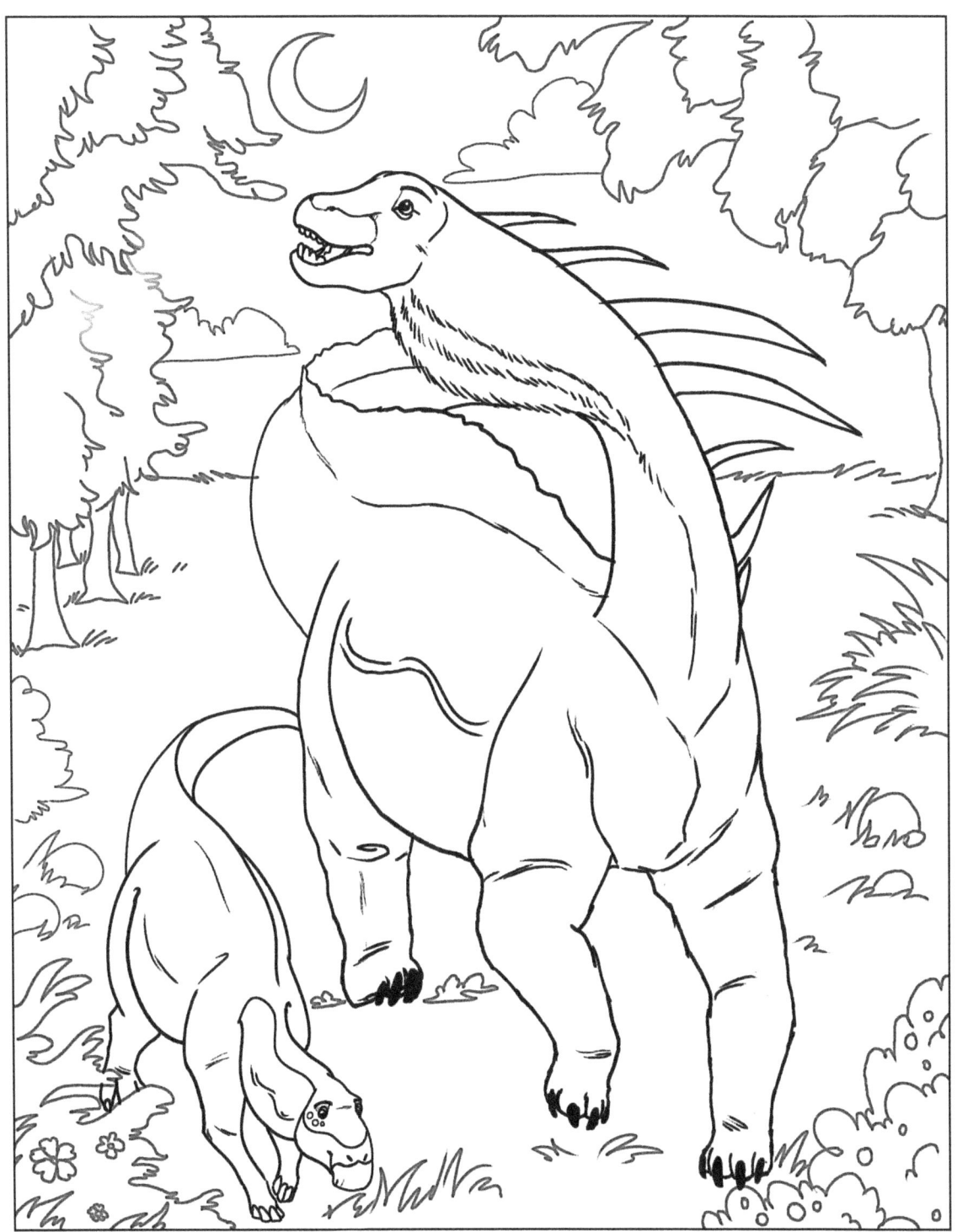

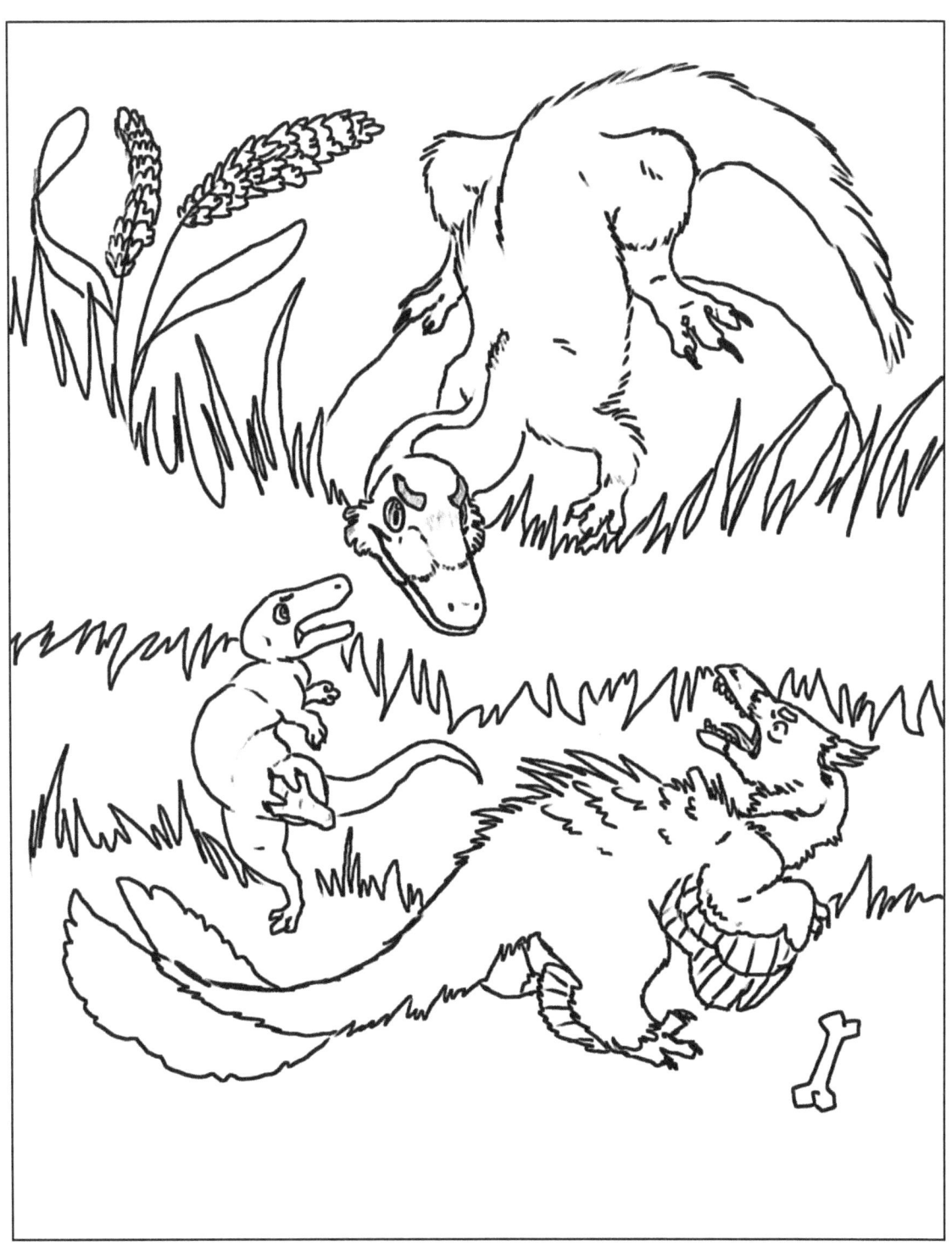

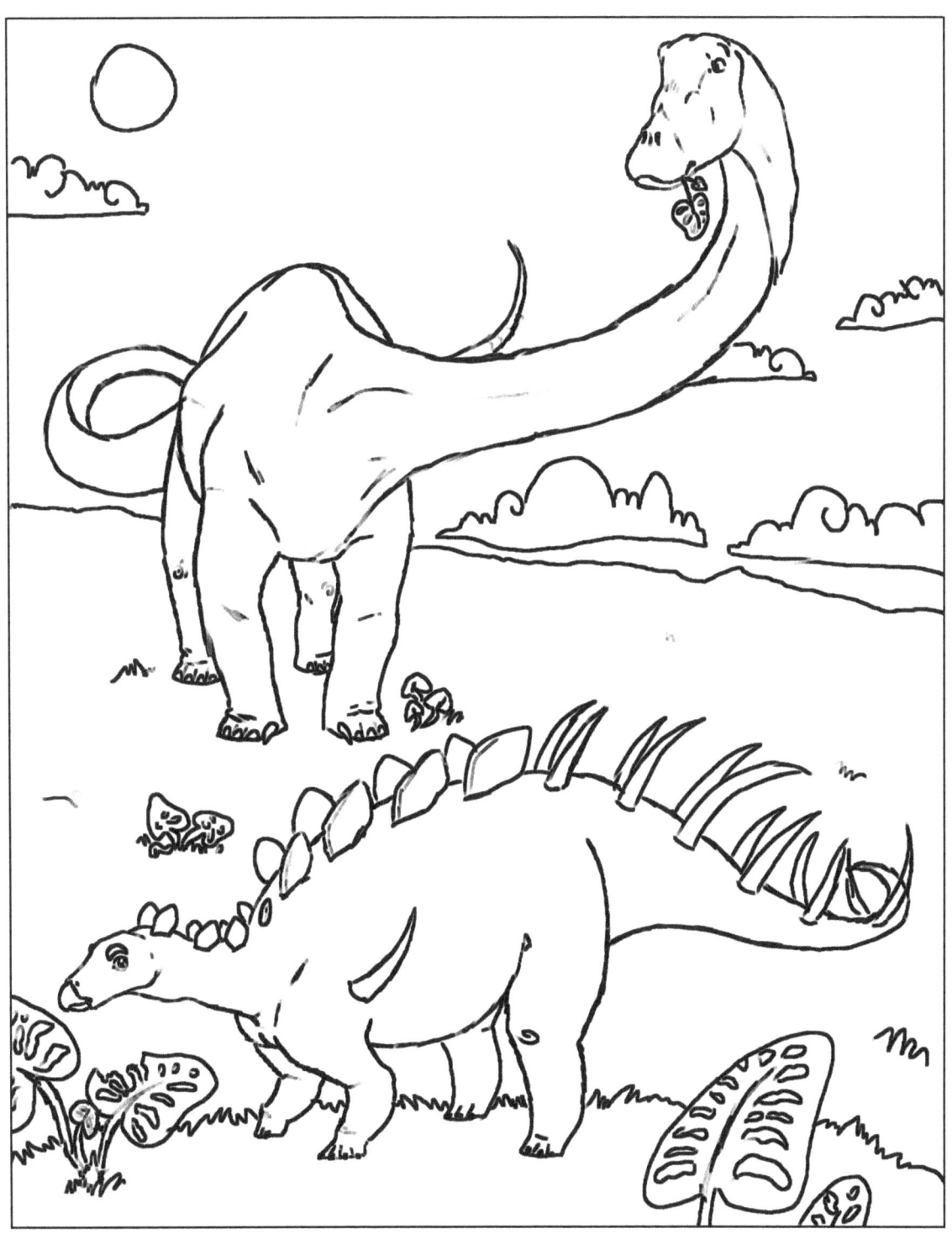

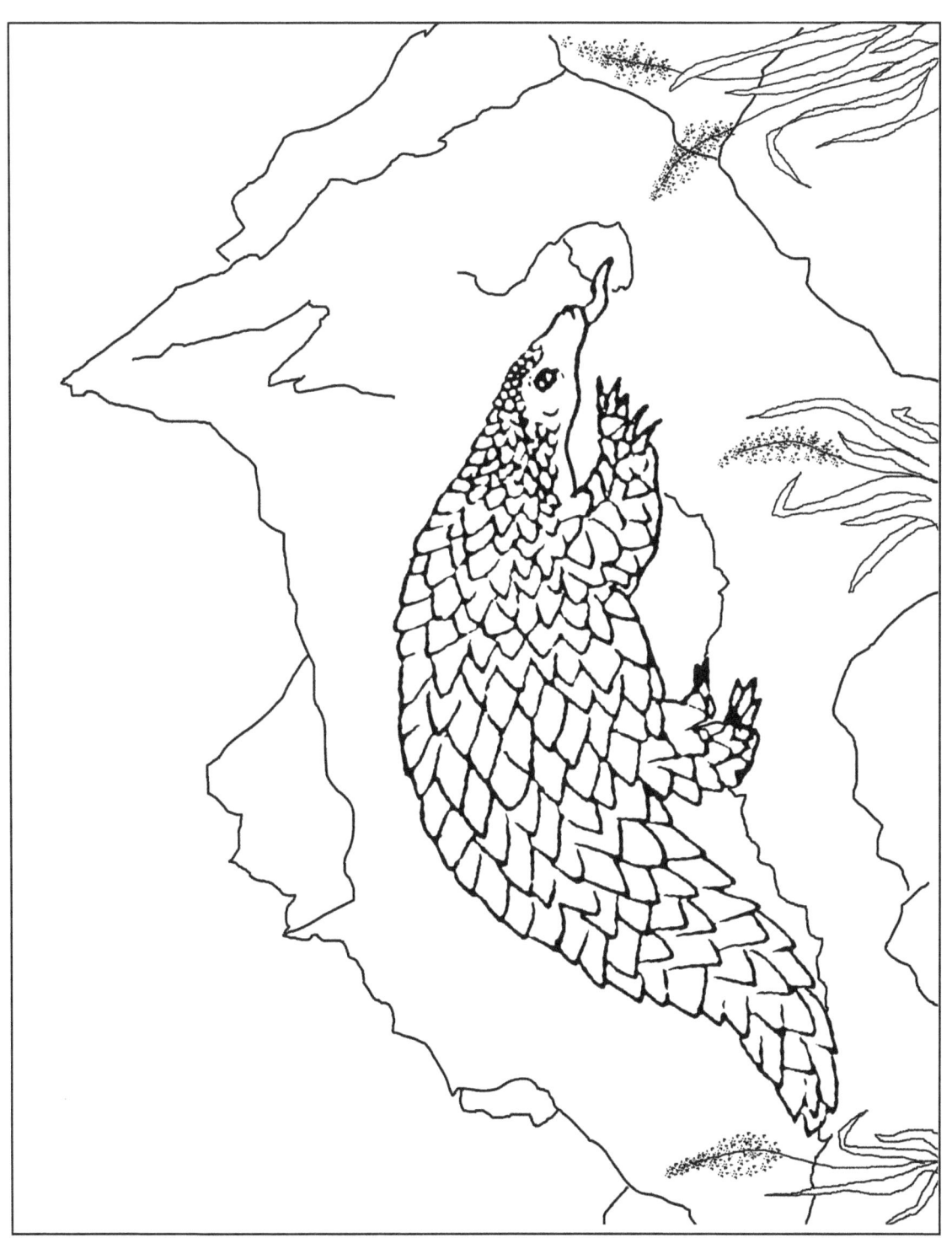

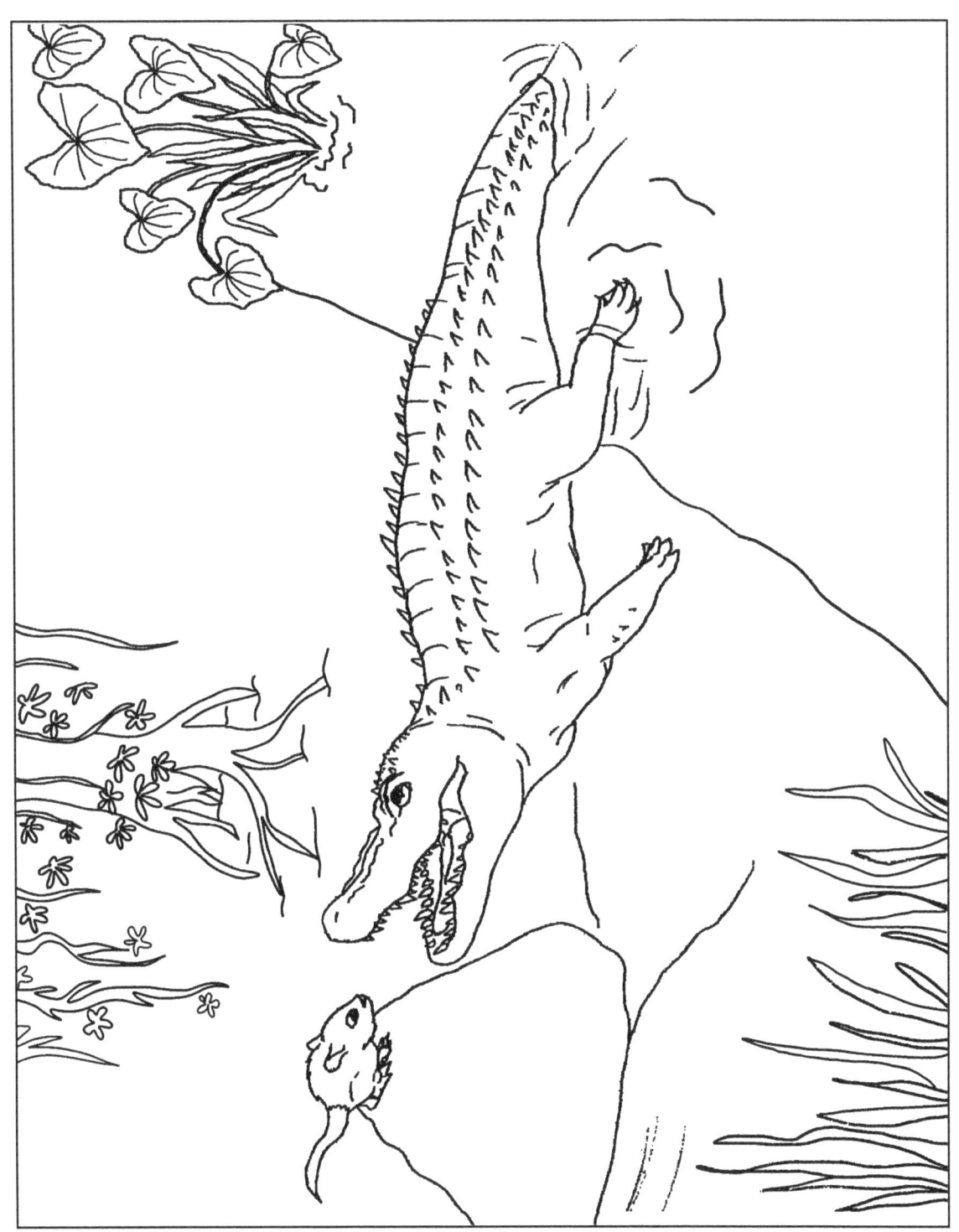

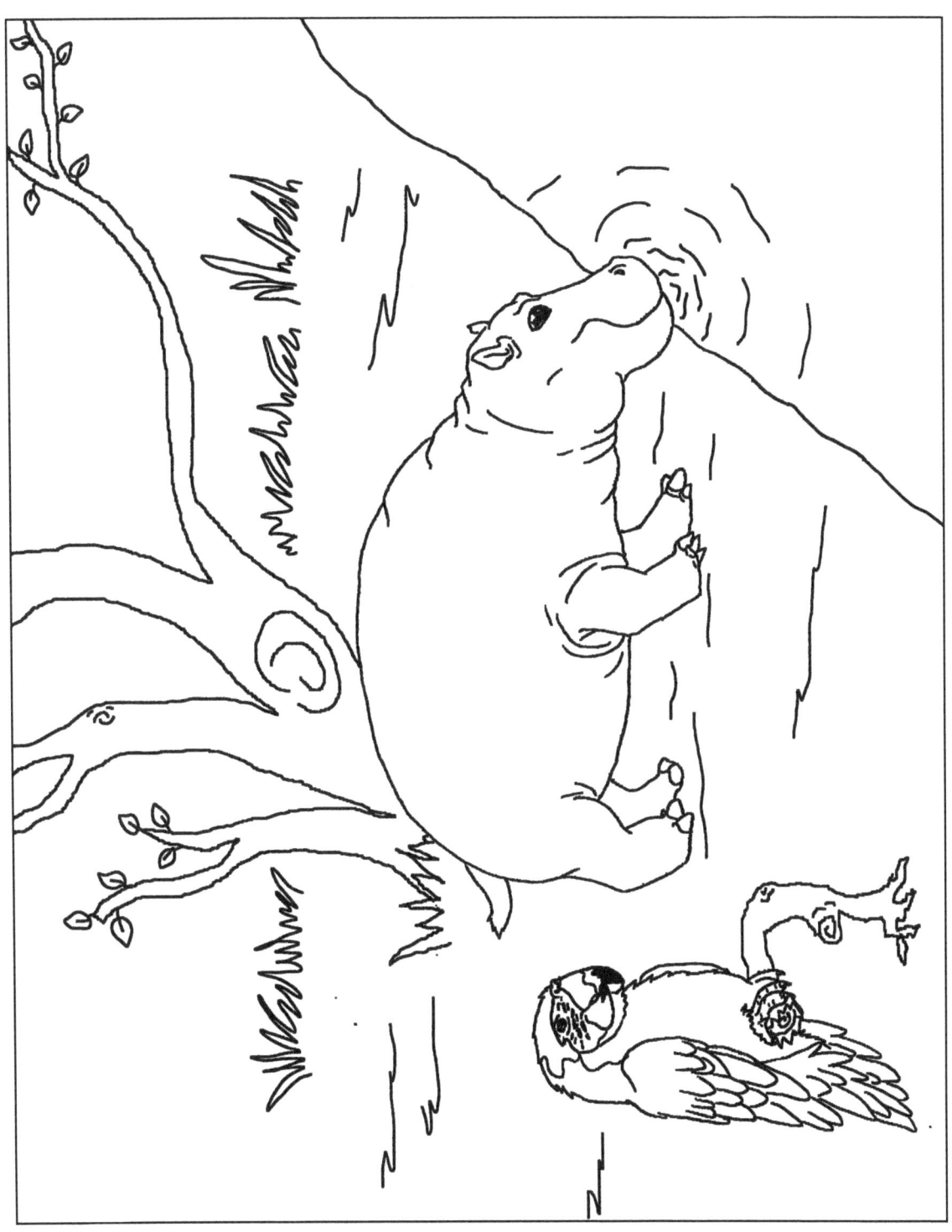

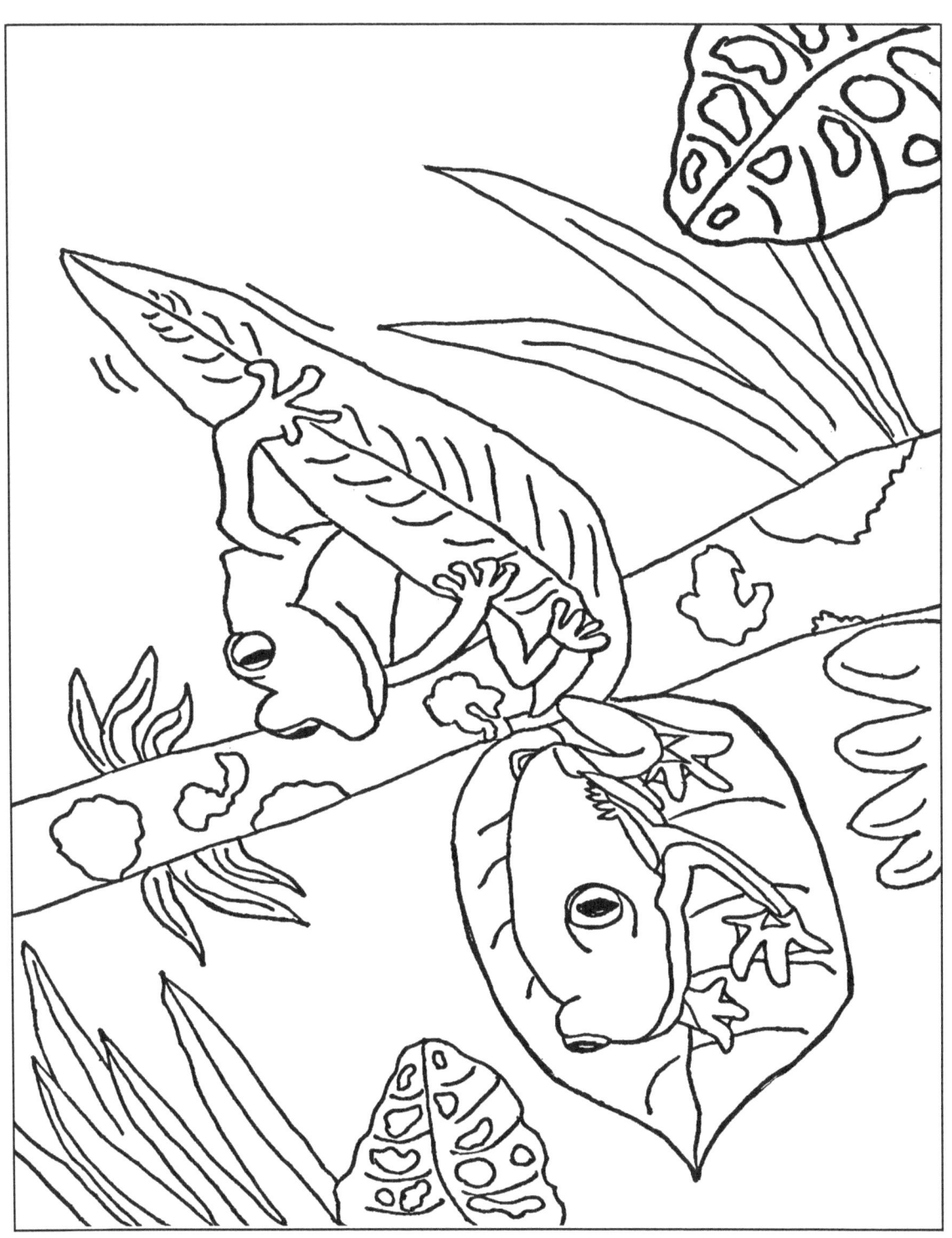

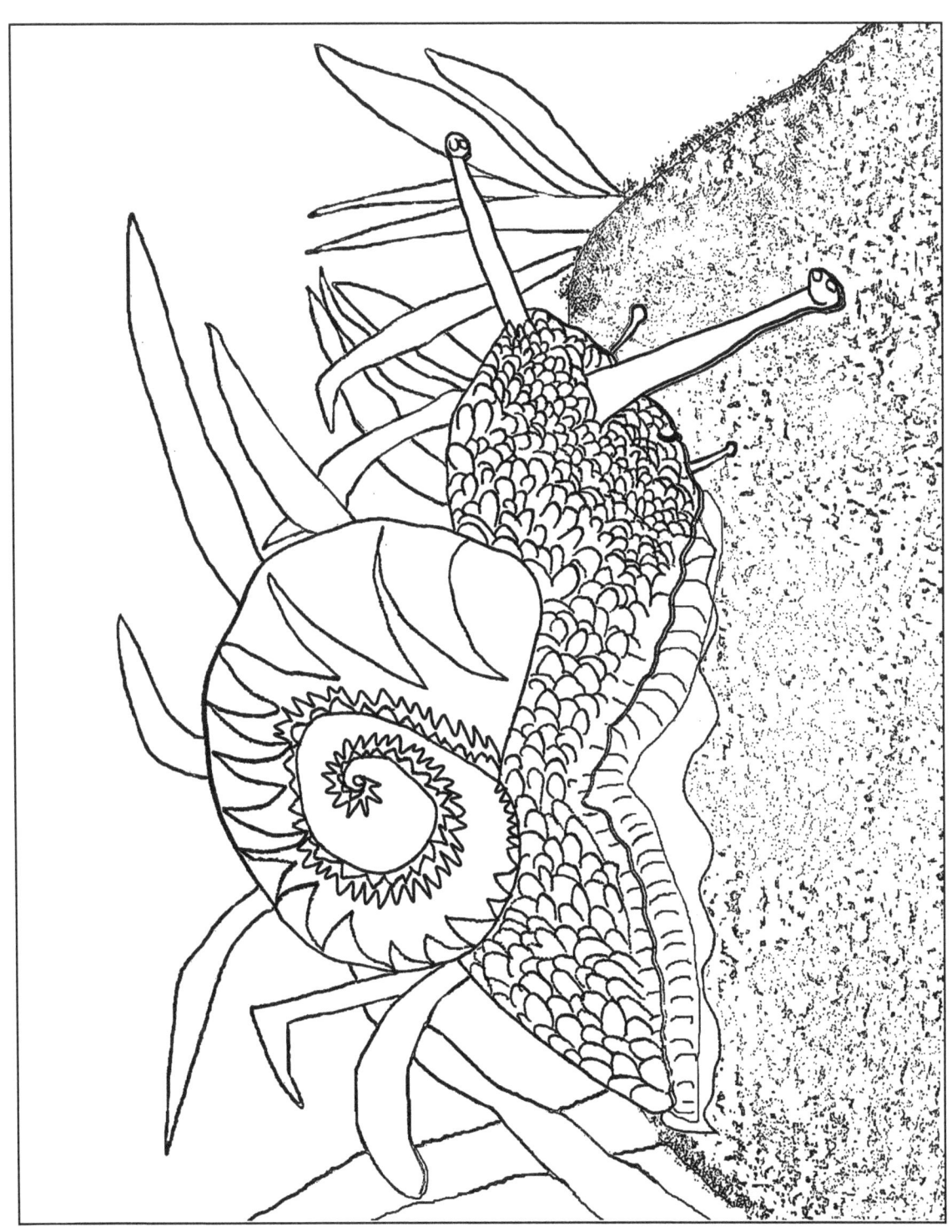

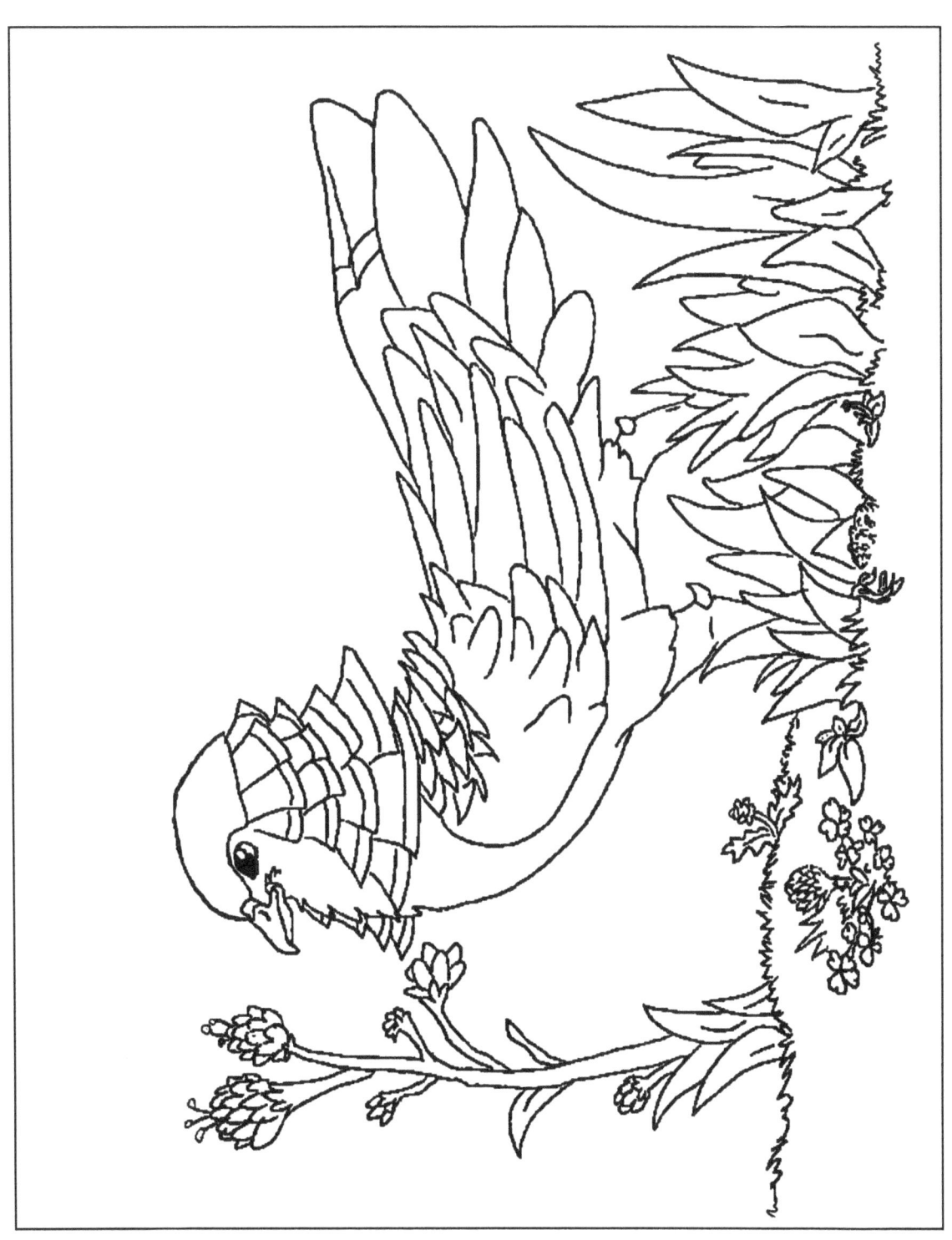

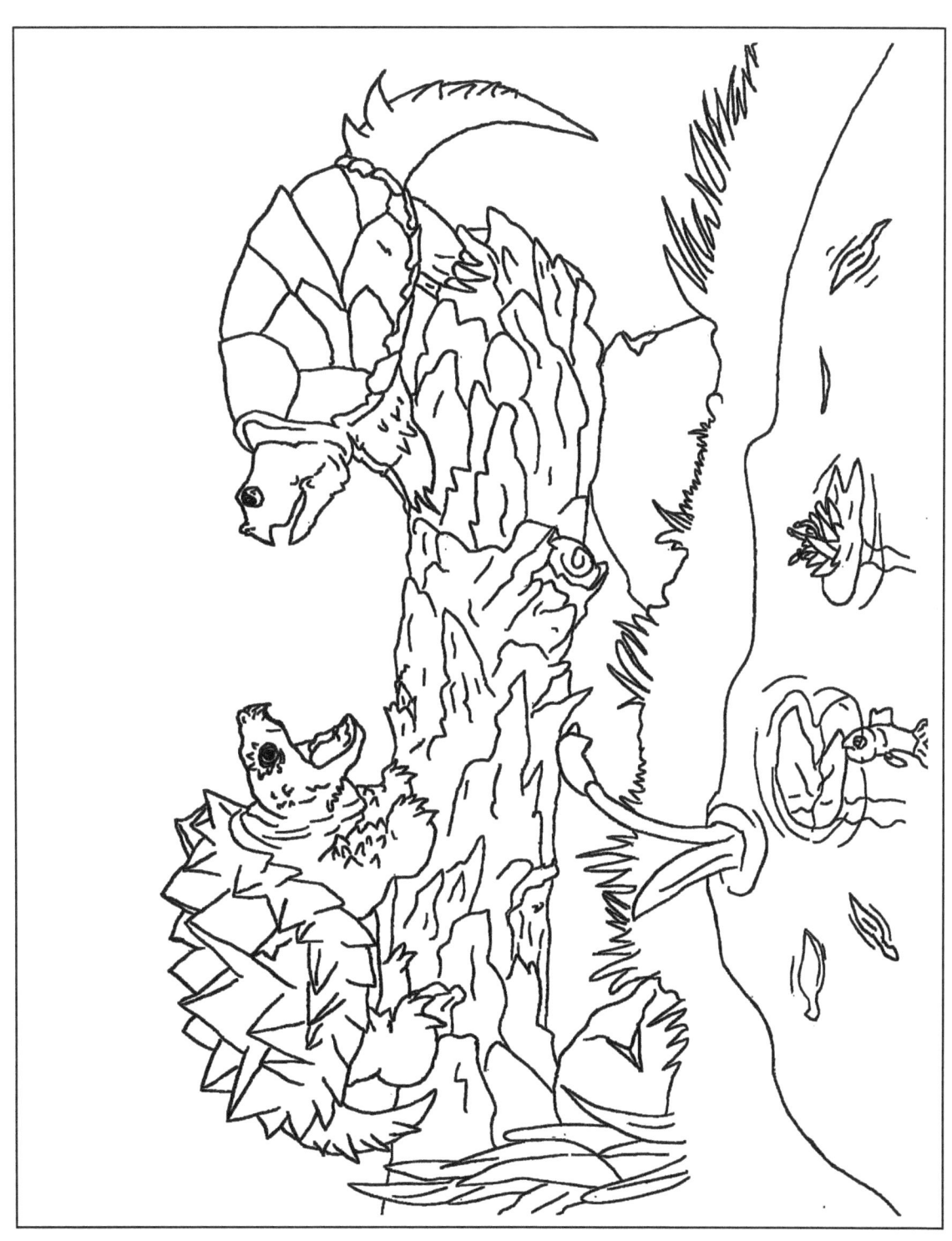

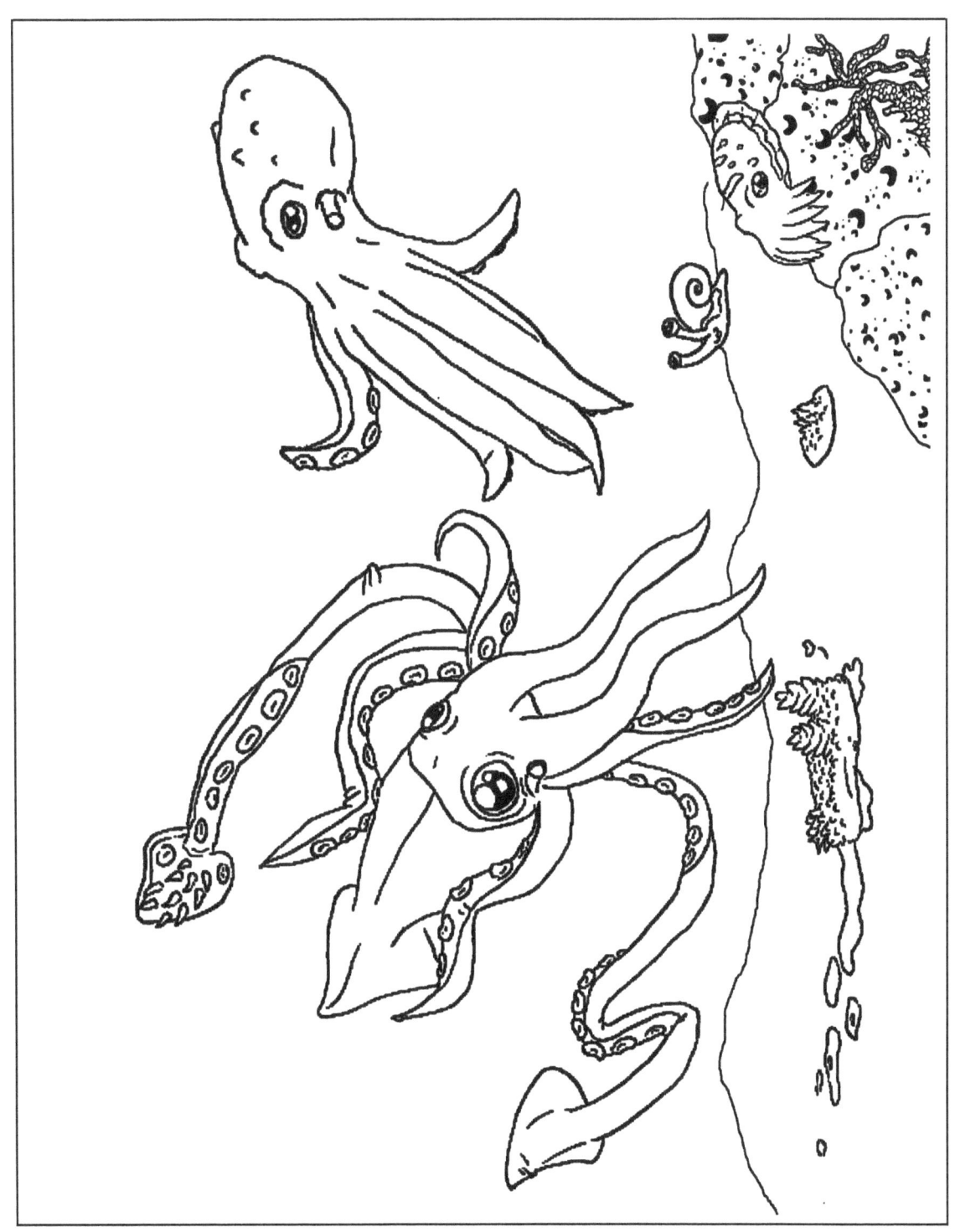

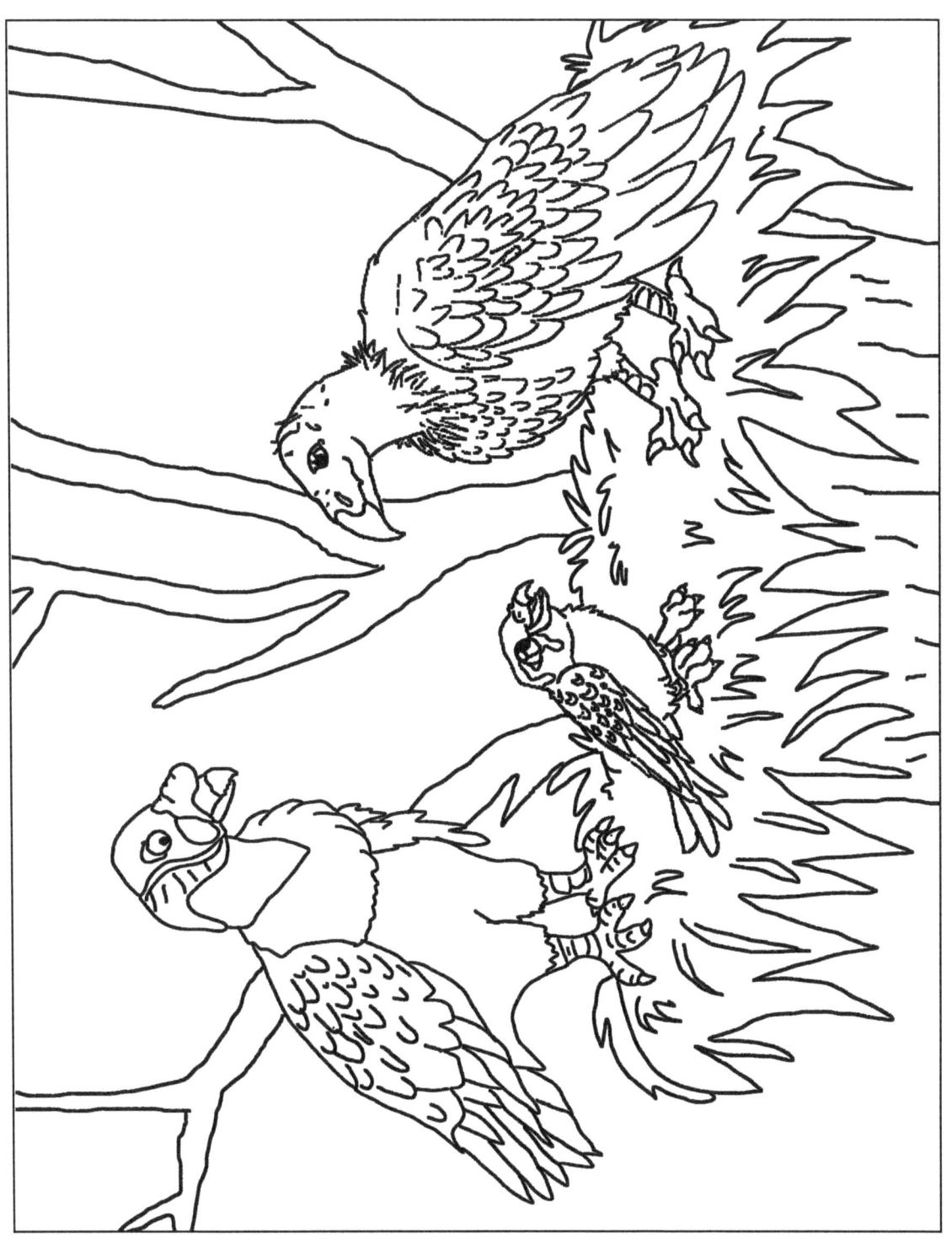

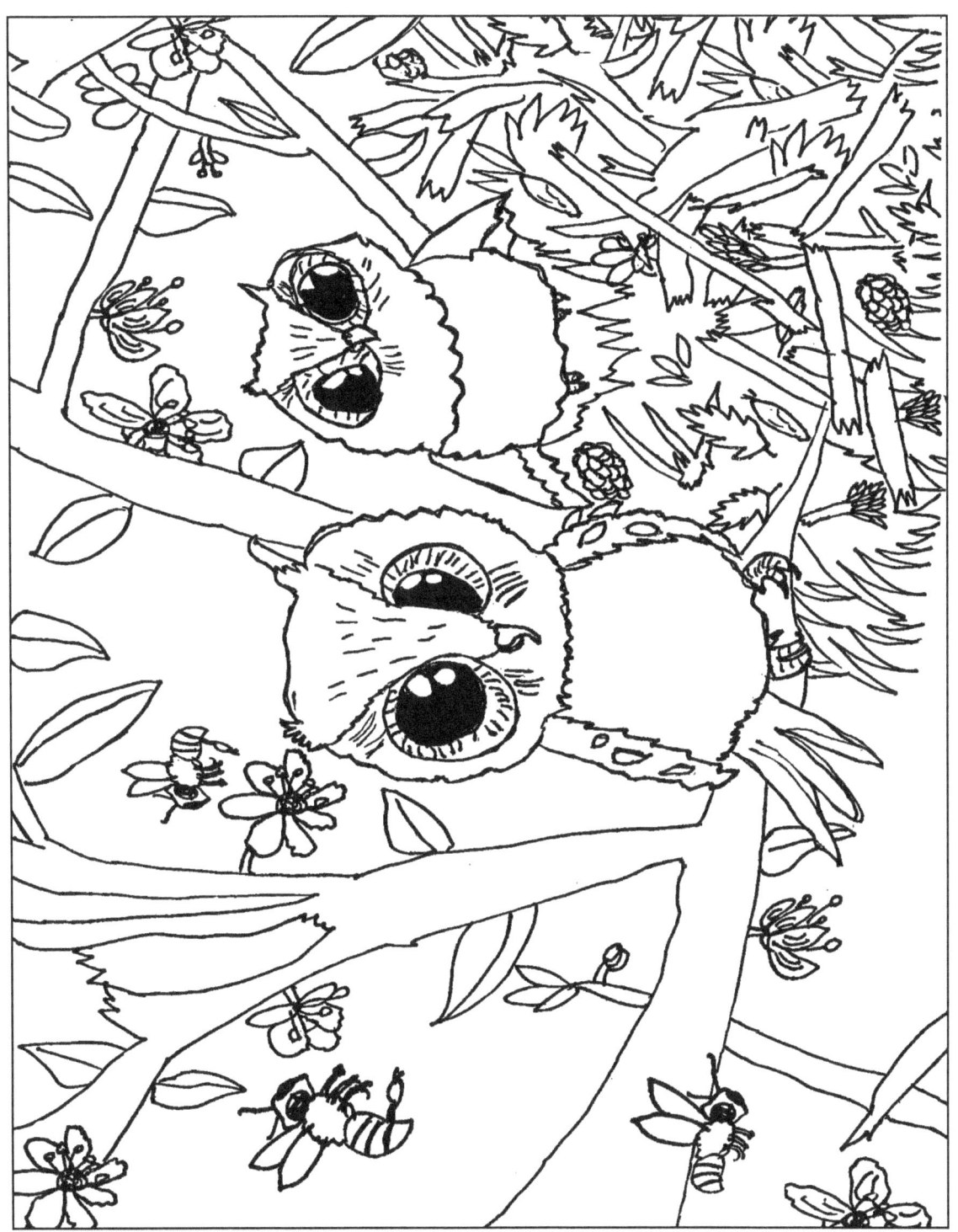

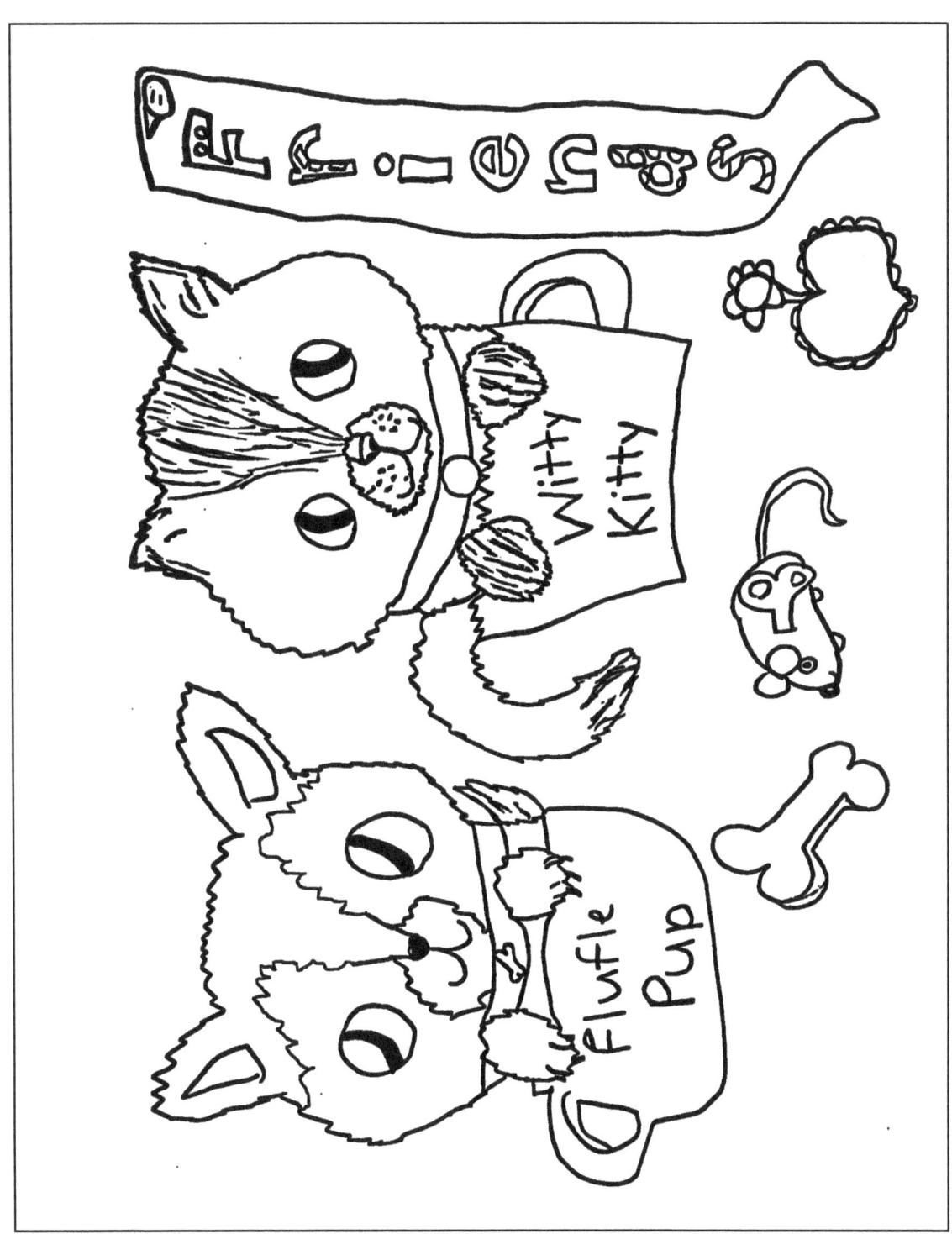

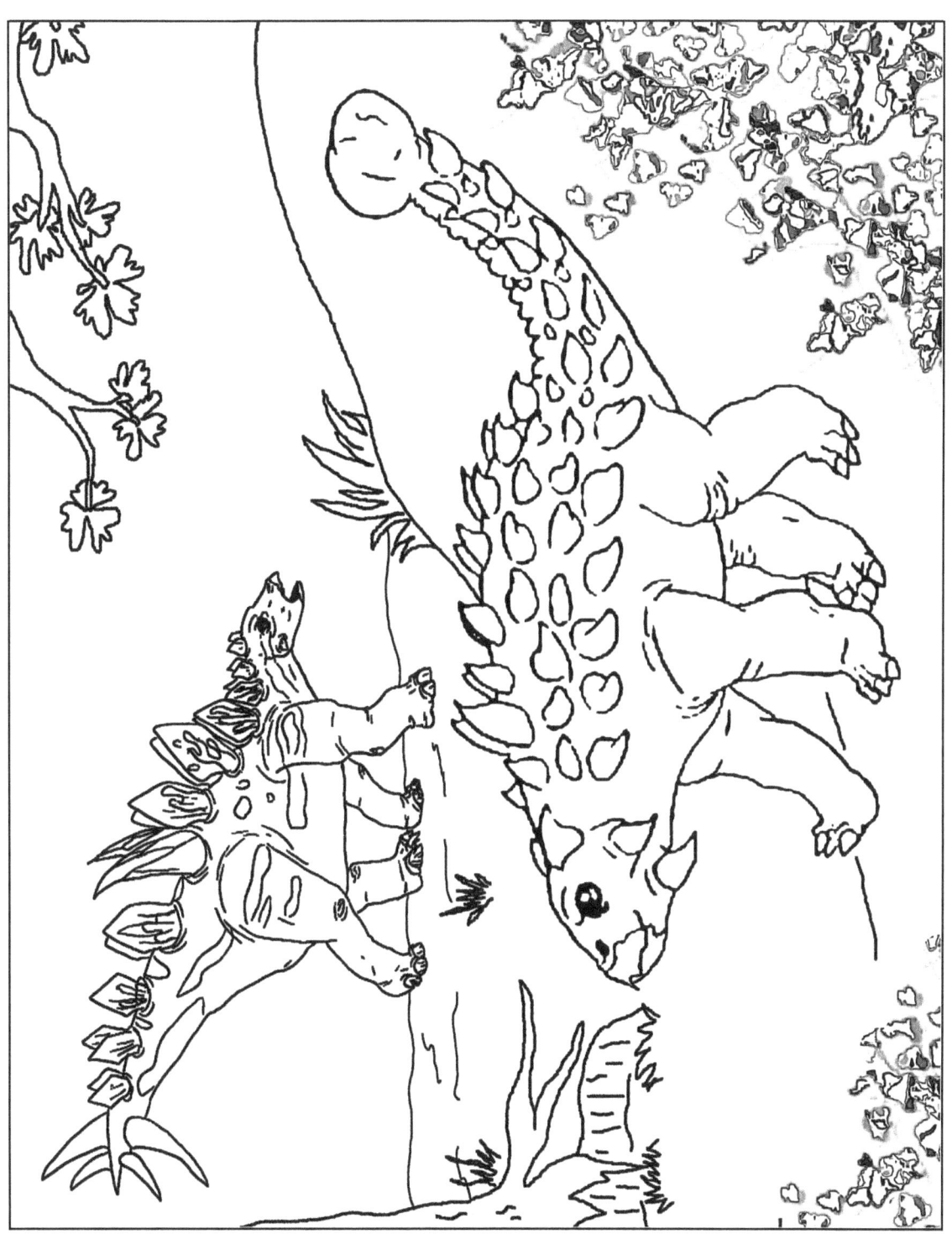

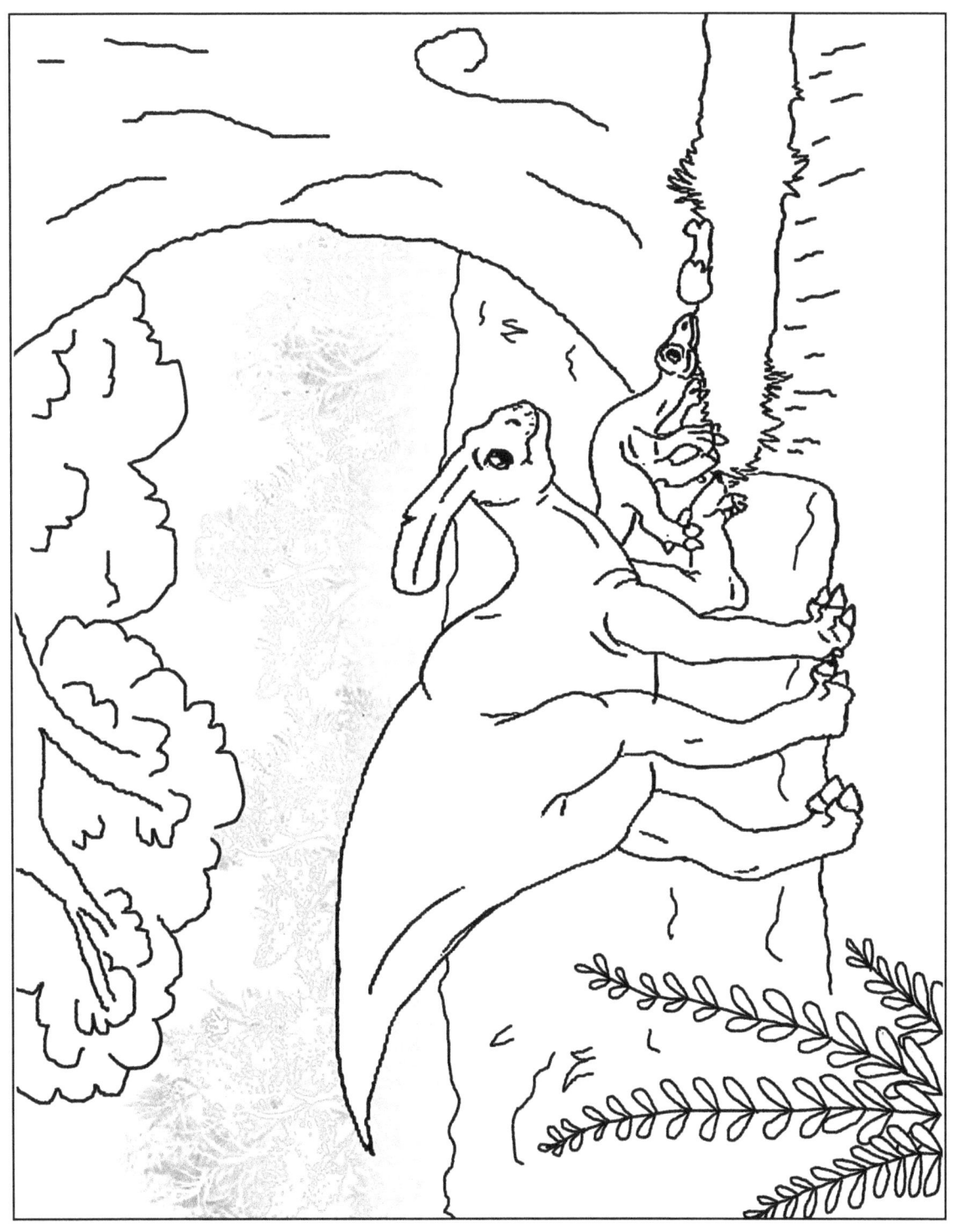

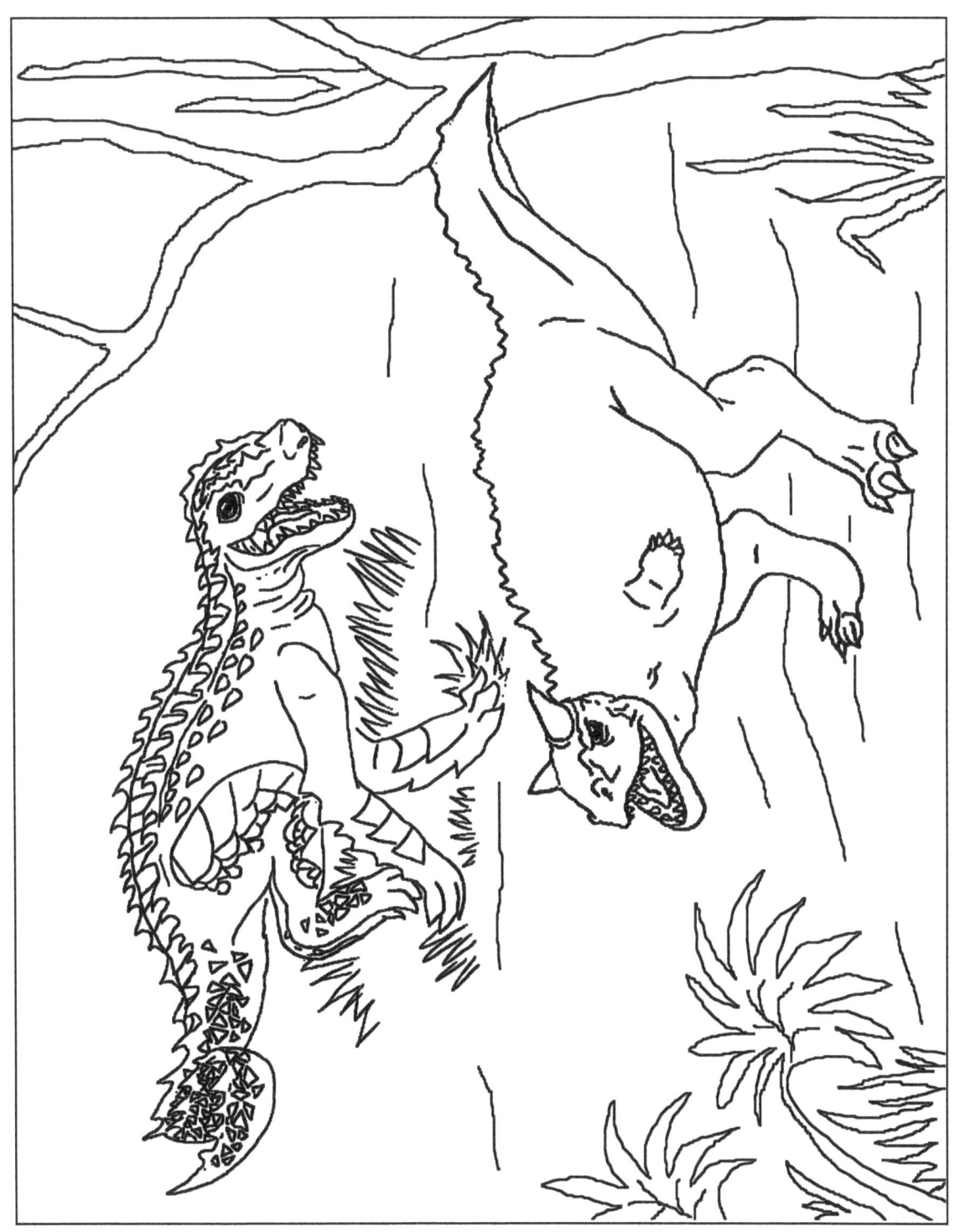

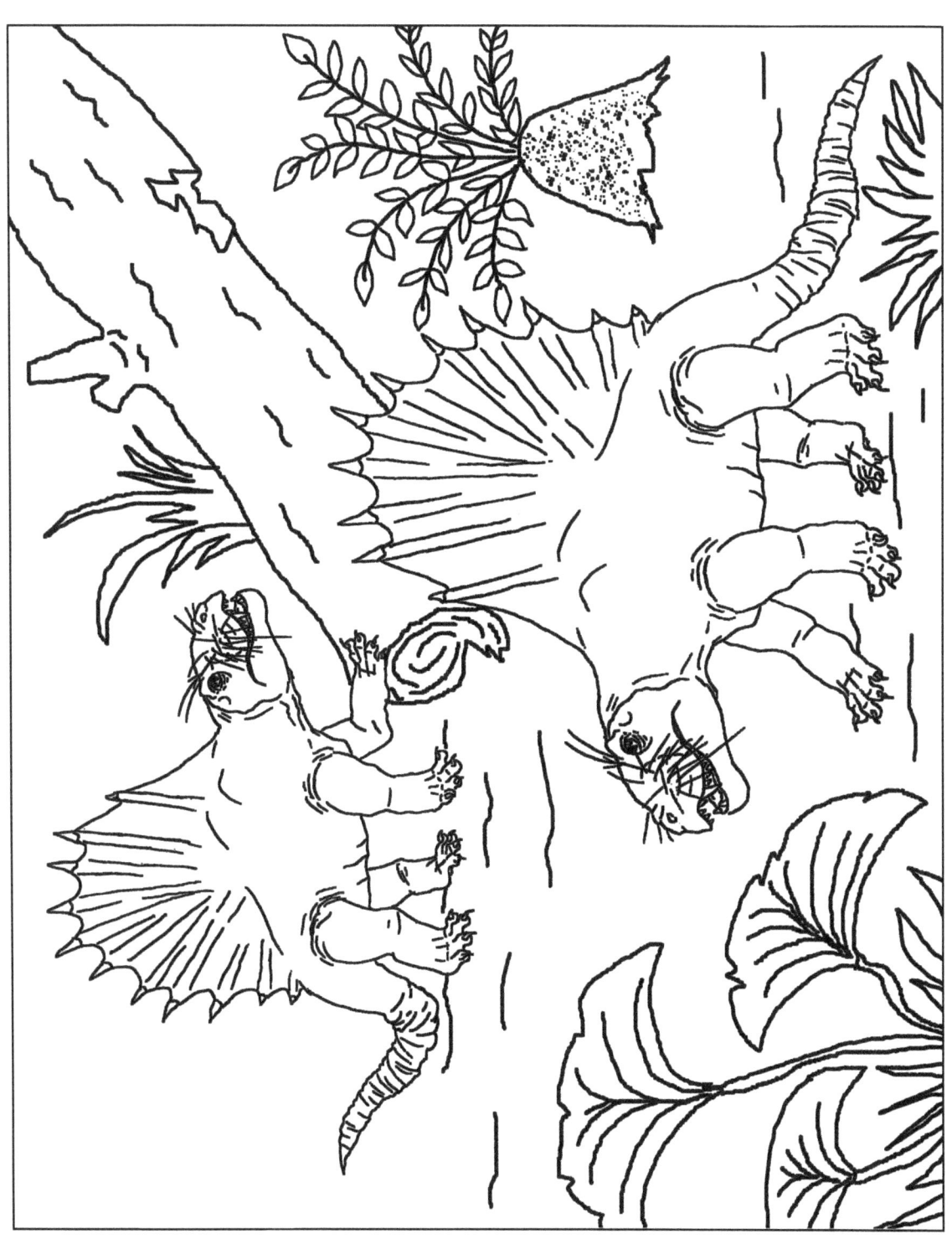

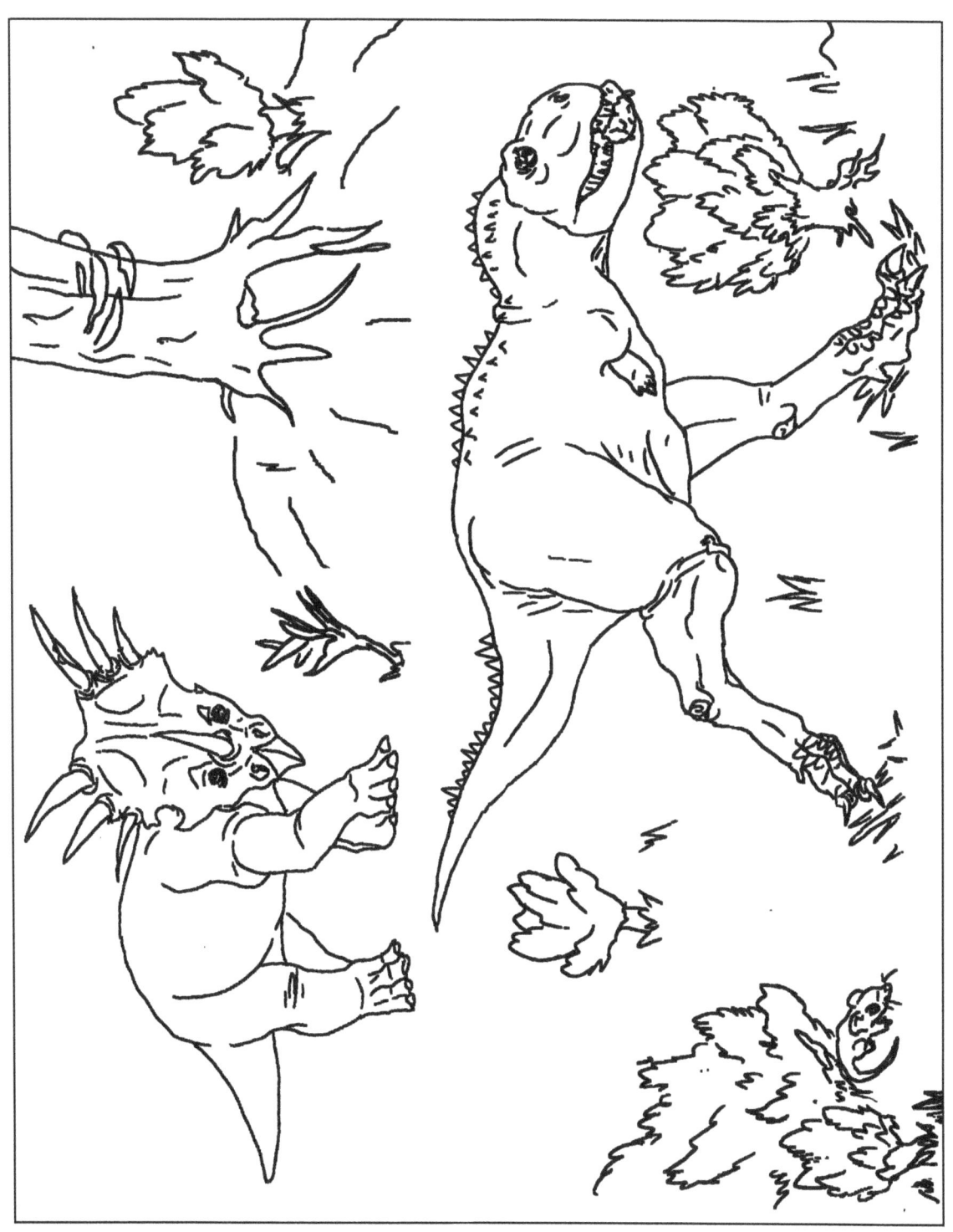

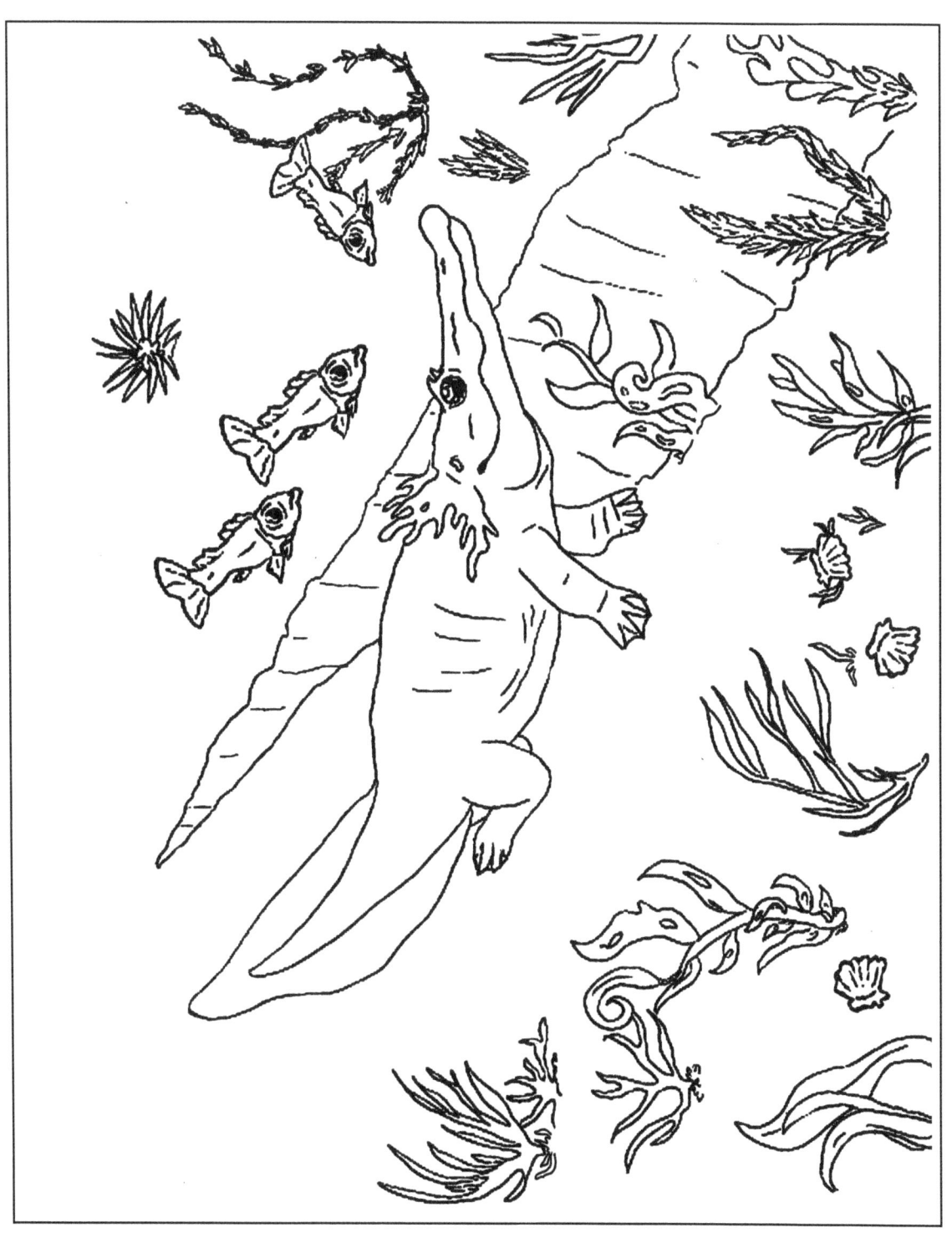

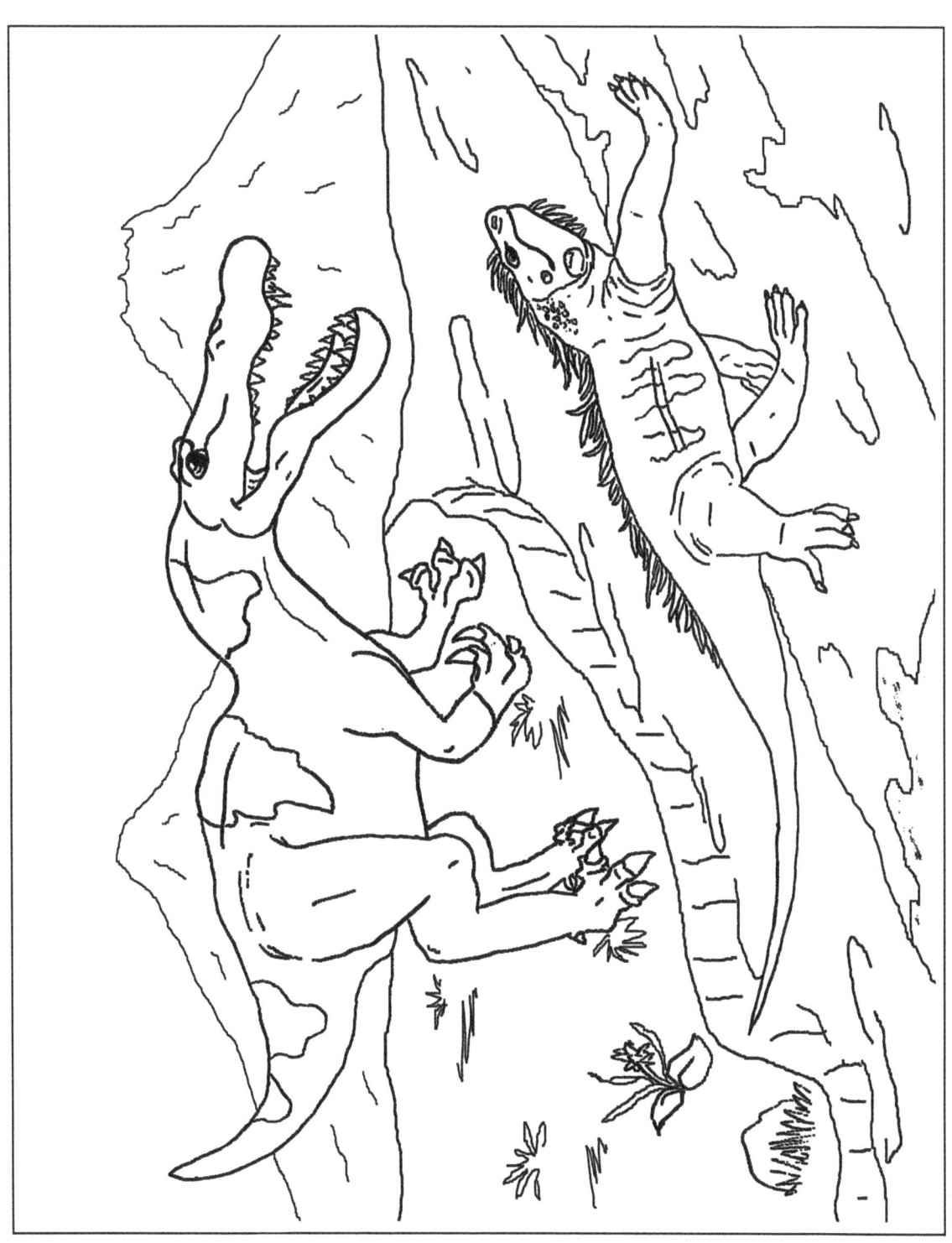

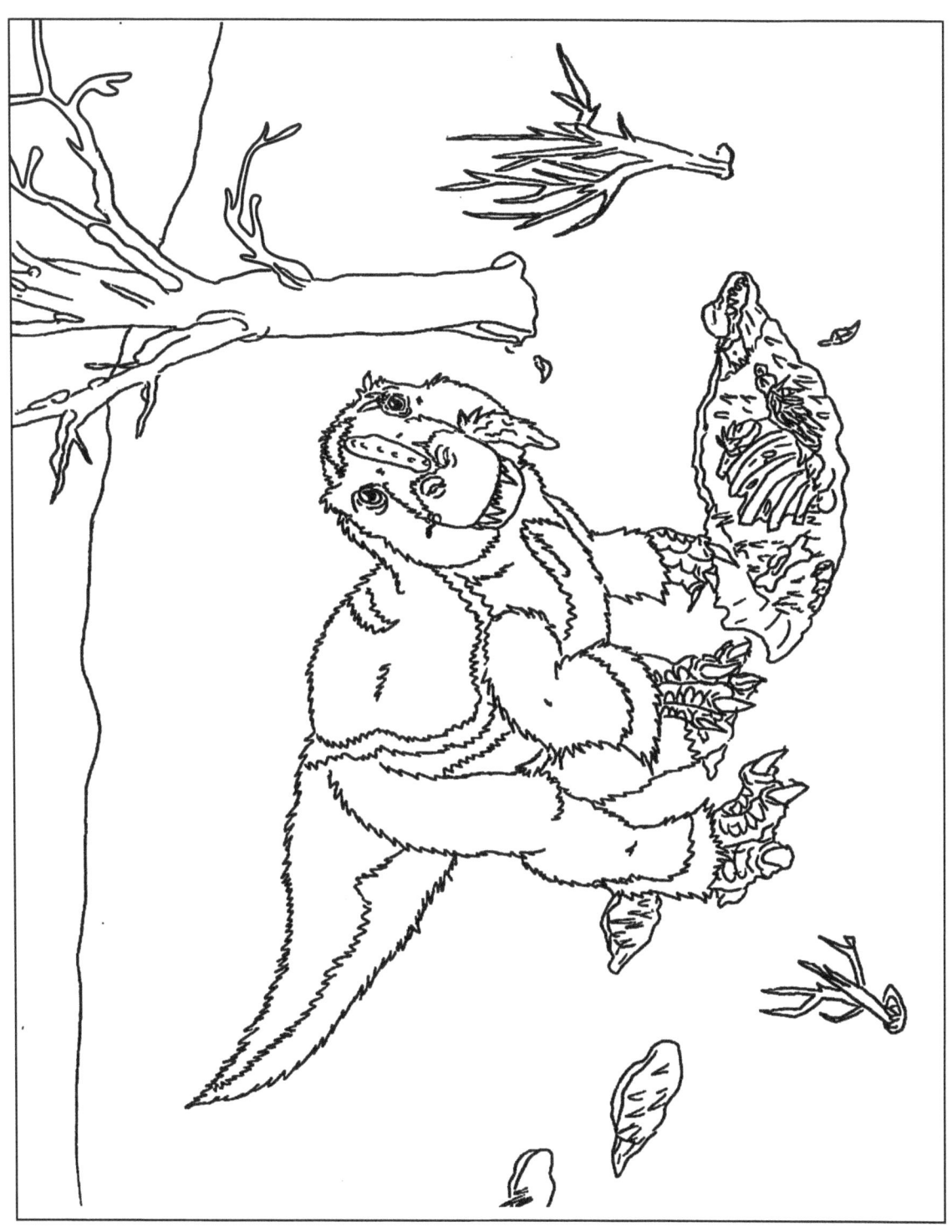

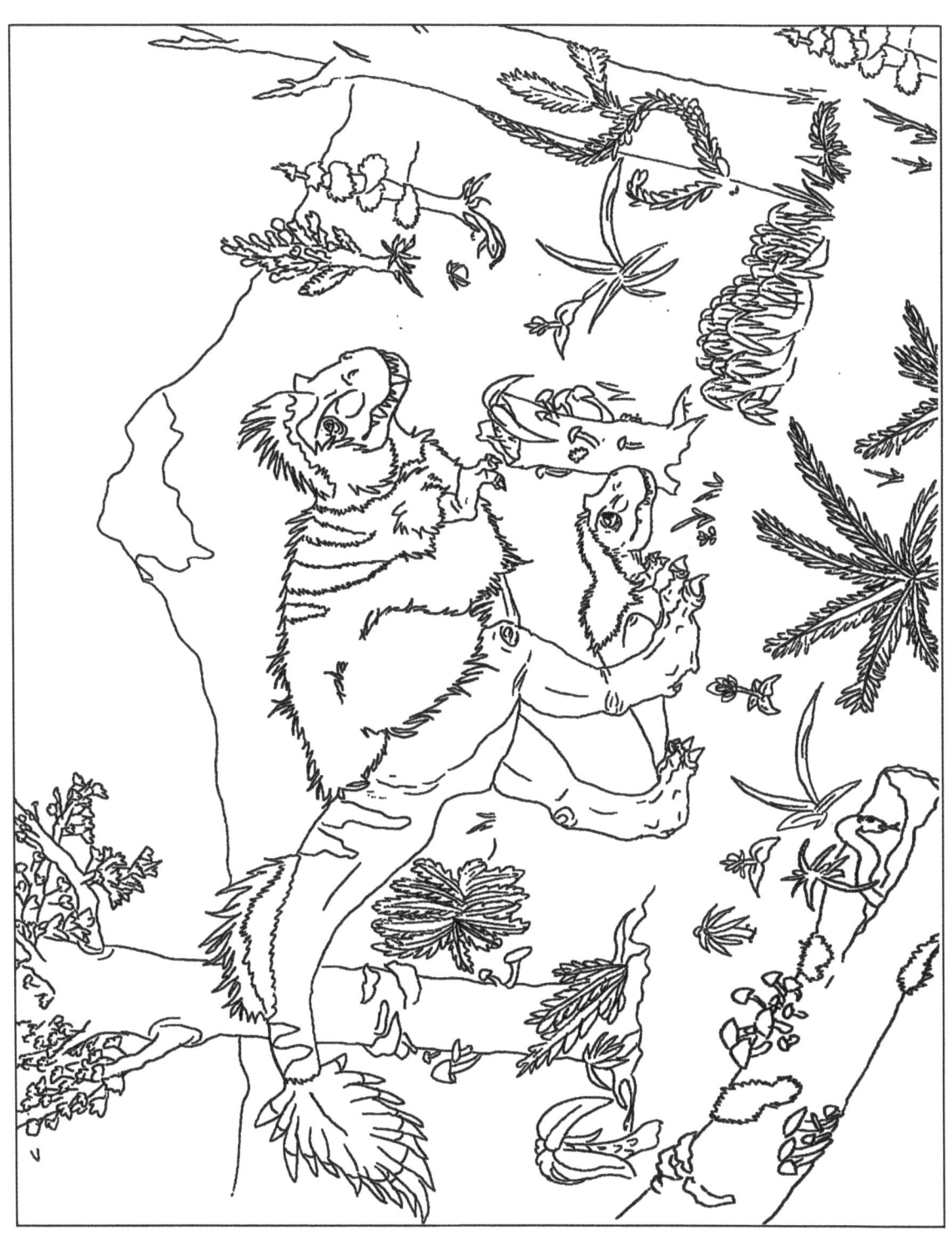

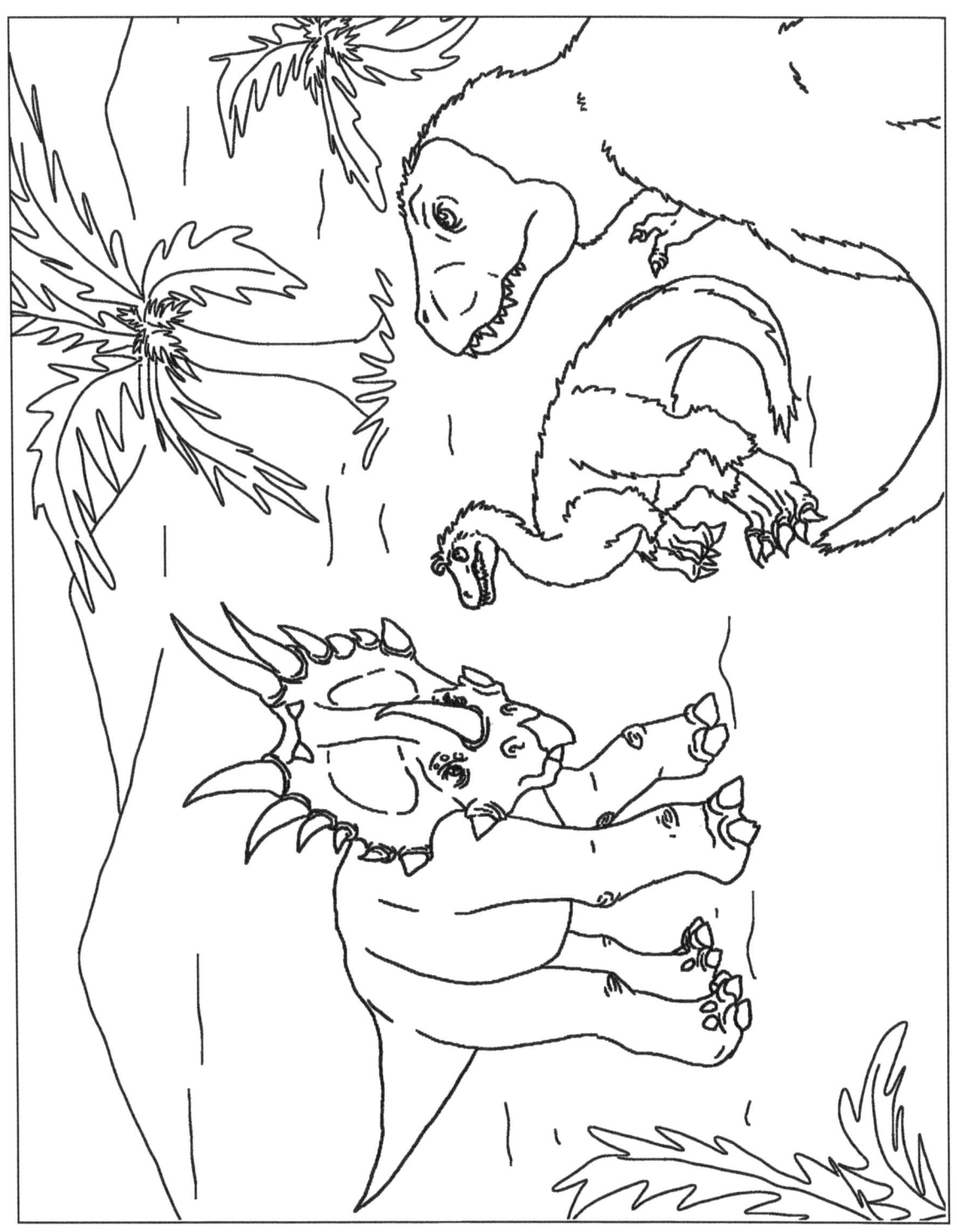

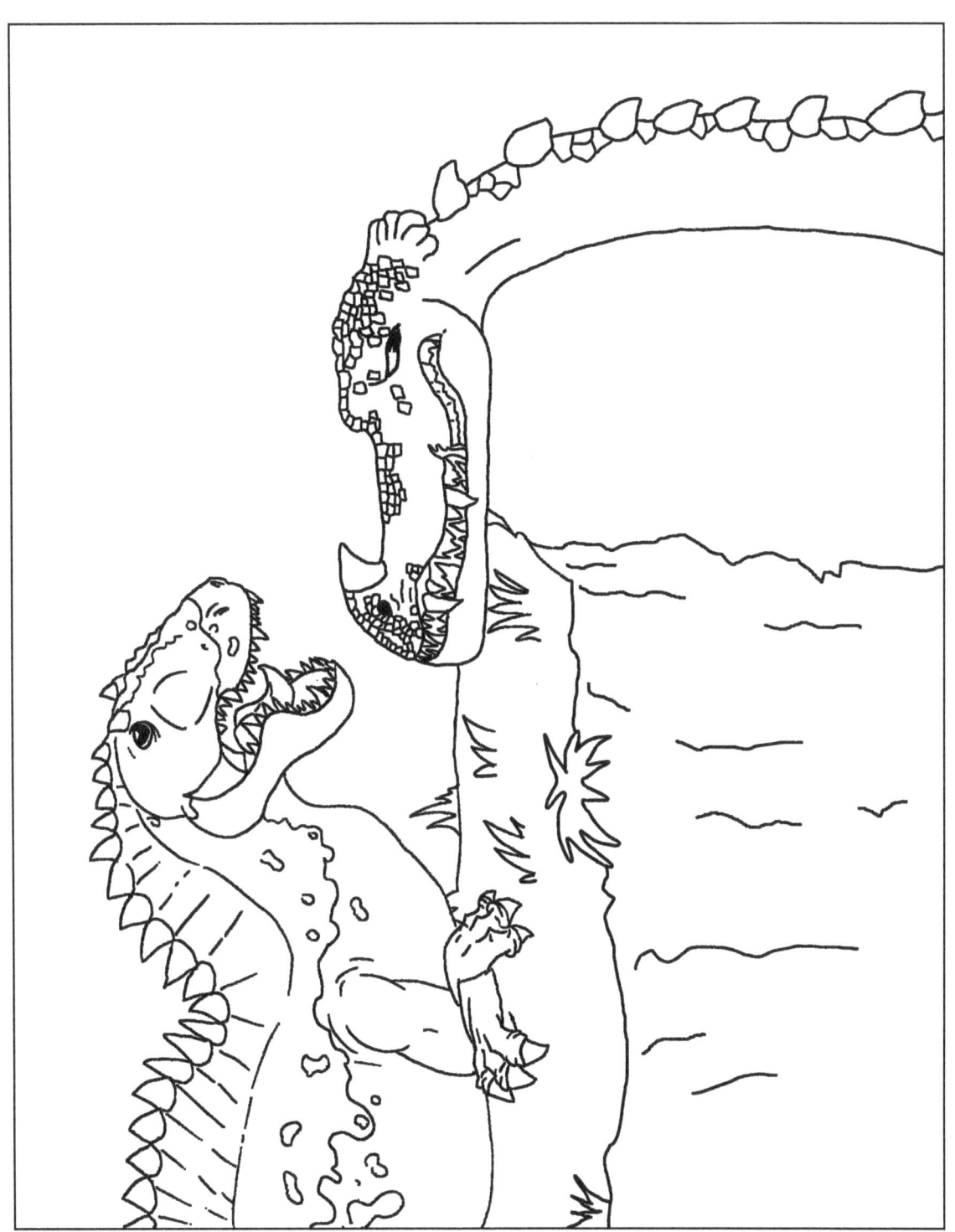

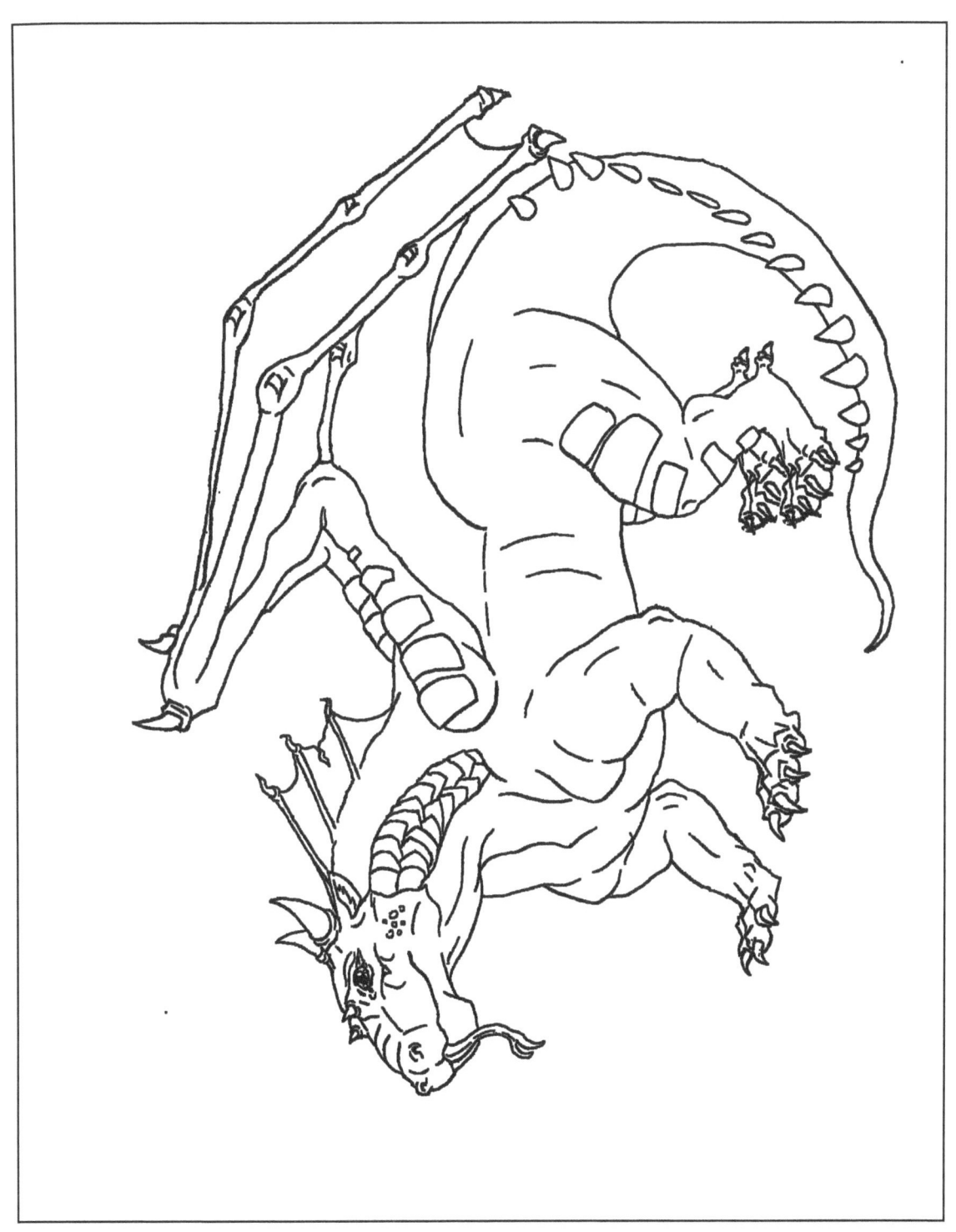

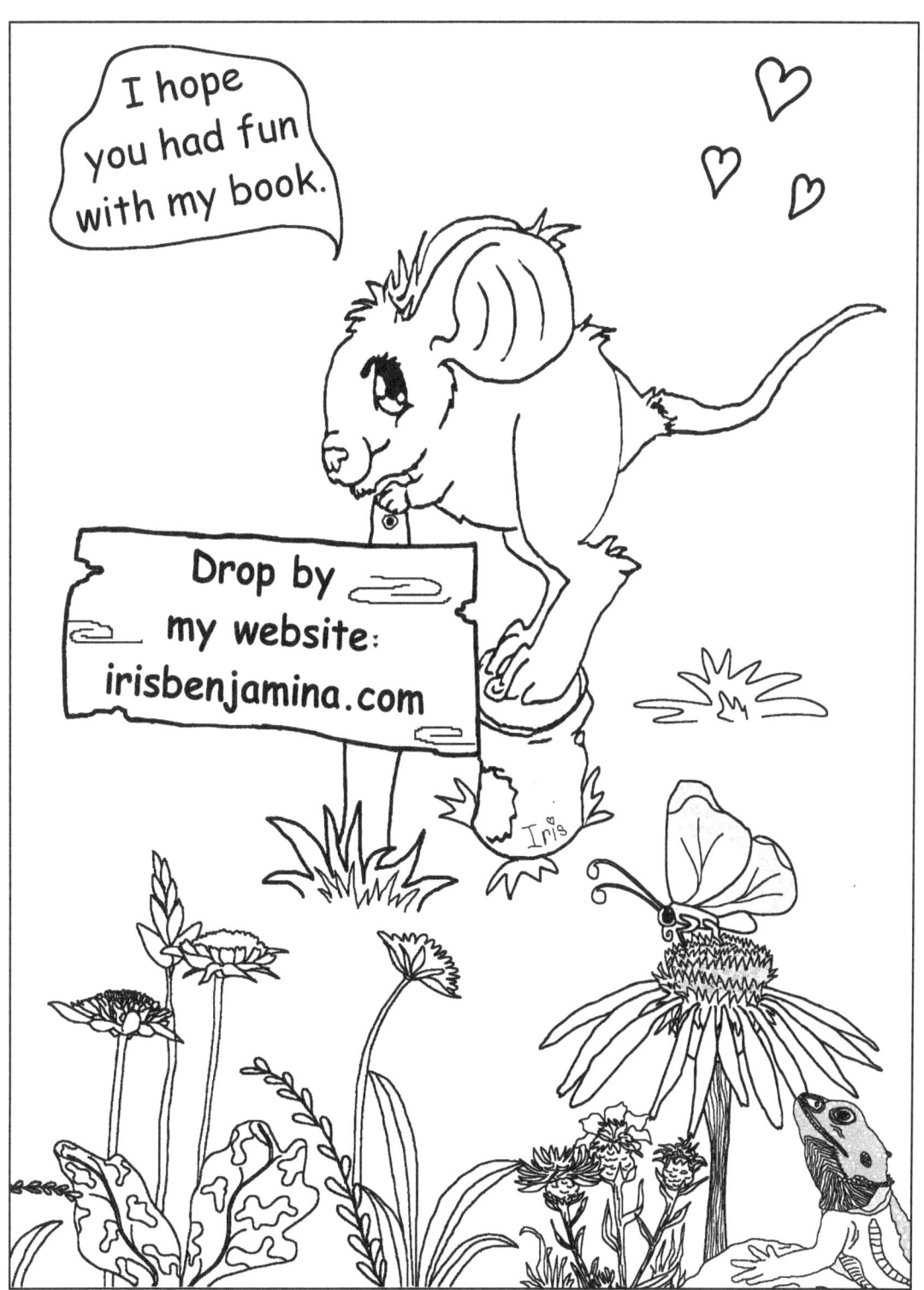